Shakyamuni Buddha's Future Prediction

HS Press

Shakyamuni Buddha's Future Prediction

INCLUDING SPIRITUAL INTERVIEW WITH
JOHN LENNON AND MESSAGES FROM
METATRON AND YAIDRON

RYUHO OKAWA

HS PRESS

Copyright © 2020 by Ryuho Okawa
English translation © Happy Science 2020
Original title: *Shakuson no Mirai Yogen*
HS Press is an imprint of IRH Press Co., Ltd.
Tokyo
ISBN 13: 978-1-943869-91-6
ISBN 10: 1-943869-91-X
Cover Image: Vit-Mar/shutterstock.com

The opinions of the spirits and space beings in this book do not necessarily reflect those of Happy Science Group.
For the mechanism behind spiritual messages, see the end section.

Contents

Preface 13

CHAPTER ONE
Shakyamuni Buddha's Future Prediction

1 Before Recording Shakyamuni Buddha's Future Prediction

The novel coronavirus problem has come to look like
The War of the Worlds 18

The spirit of John Lennon said, "It's Divine Will, so it
can't be helped" 20

Daring to ask Shakyamuni Buddha, who chooses his words
carefully, about his predictions for the future 22

2 Now Is the Time to Think about a World Ruled by Death

"You cannot build the future as an extension of the
present" 24

Now is an age when you must consider the meaning of
death 26

What if the situation in New York occurs in other places
worldwide? 28

How many people would be infected or die if the current
conditions in Japan were the global standard? 30

A modern witch hunt could also occur 33

"If this world becomes more like a Utopia, the population
will be allowed to grow" 35

3 Now Is the Last Chance for Humankind to Change Direction

A time of population increase is also a time when a savior's power weakens 38

Humankind still has some time to think 39

Preach how human beings should be and fight to prevent a future controlled by AI 42

If humans don't notice now, something worse might come 45

4 Why Is the Virus Spreading?

The virus symbolizes all of humankind 48

It depends on whether or not Japan itself can acquire enough power to save the world 51

Cross-cultural contact causes epidemics 53

It depends on whether or not you can spread Buddha's Truth wider and faster and turn it into a trend 56

5 What Is Required of Us Now

Thinking about "what is required of us now" from the perspective of future generations 59

One factor behind the spread of coronavirus infections is humanity's self-punishment 62

When you pray to the True God, you will know the True God 65

You must realize that not knowing yourself is a sin 67

6 Future Developments in International Affairs and Japan's Mission

The Great East Japan Earthquake toppled the DPJ-led administration 69

Japan should have political, economic, and diplomatic systems that are independent of China 70

China will suffer repercussions for causing this global viral outbreak 72

Shakyamuni's views on the possibility of a U.S.-China war over coronavirus infections 73

Japan should create a national defense system that enables it to defend itself 75

Japan's prerequisites for expressing opinions about the religious conflicts in the world 77

7 The Spiritual Backgrounds behind World Religions and Their Problems

The guidance from Elohim and Hermes lay at the root of the establishment of Islam 81

Now is the age when a third power must develop 84

Points to reflect on in modern Christianity and Islam 86

Now is also the perfect time for a world religion to develop 88

8 People Are Being Tested to See Whether or Not They Have True Faith

The battle between light and darkness and the age of chaos will continue for some time 91

How should we think about miracles? 94

The God of Genesis will never succumb to bat venom 97

First, produce 10 times the number of true believers in Japan ... 100

CHAPTER TWO

Spiritual Messages from John Lennon

1 **The Spirit of John Lennon Talks about the World's Future**

   A smaller population will lead to fewer wars 104

   The novel coronavirus and YouTube are similar 107

   Coronavirus: an alarm to awaken people to the truth that everything passes by? 110

   "There's no way you can protect yourself with a cloth mask" 114

2 **The Idea That a Population Decline Would Bring World Peace**

   The coronavirus will spread on Chinese navy vessels and nullify military power 116

   In the eyes of the heavenly world, worthless things are popular in this world 120

   Are viruses the shadow of the minds of humans, who have multiplied too much? 124

3 Rock and Roll for Humankind, Who Have Little Faith

The higher the population, the higher the number of nonbelievers 128

The world is getting tougher on people 130

What if John Lennon were to sing rock now? 132

What will happen to the leaders of the U.S., U.K., and Germany? 136

A world in which John Lennon was shot dead must not continue to prosper 140

4 Heaven's Will in the Eyes of the Spirit of John Lennon

"The population won't grow so much anymore" 144

"In the end, space people will begin to attack from outer space" 146

The civilization based on reason and intelligence is about to bring an end to humanity 148

Bad people need to reflect on themselves 151

The trigger and purpose of this turmoil 154

CHAPTER THREE

Messages from Metatron and Yaidron

- UFO Reading 50 -

1 **Message from Metatron**

"We are also one of the variables" "I'm going to put an artistic end to this" 164

Happy Science must be the last stronghold 167

2 **Message from Yaidron**

Fear not the coronavirus 170

People in Western countries and the Middle East will seek for the Real God 173

There exists the Original God of not only the Earth, but the universe 175

We are also fighting to prevent the future of the Earth from becoming confused 178

3 **"Spiritual Messages from Shakyamuni Buddha" Revealed a Part of the True Thoughts of El Cantare** ... 182

Afterword 185

About the Author 187
What Is El Cantare? 188
What Is a Spiritual Message? 190
About Happy Science 194
About Happy Science Movies 198
Contact Information 200
About Happiness Realization Party 202
About IRH Press 203
Books by Ryuho Okawa 204
Music by Ryuho Okawa 213

In this book, there are a total of five interviewers from Happy Science, symbolized as A, B, C, D, and E, in the order that they first appear.

Preface

In Chapter One, we received some future predictions from Shakyamuni Buddha, which is unusual for him, about the ongoing coronavirus pandemic.

From his views and predictions, I am sure you will see his opinions as very orthodox for a religious leader. I and definitely many others have become fed up with the array of attachments to physical life in this world that we see or hear in various newspaper reports and television news coverage.

The orders issued by the government and municipal leaders seem like trying to drive away a swarm of ants with a stick. If you are completely repulsed by these sorts of materialistic, worldly politics, then reading Chapter Two, a spiritual message from the "rocking" John Lennon, might make you feel better.

At any rate, the proliferation of godless humans is at a turning point.

Ryuho Okawa
Master & CEO of Happy Science Group
April 23, 2020

CHAPTER ONE

Shakyamuni Buddha's Future Prediction

*Originally recorded in Japanese on April 14, 2020,
in the Special Lecture Hall of Happy Science in Japan,
and later translated into English.*

Shakyamuni Buddha (Gautama Siddhartha)

The founder of Buddhism, who was born about 2,500 or 2,600 years ago in the area now known as Nepal. He was born to *Suddhodana*, the king of the *Shakya* clan, who ruled a nearby kingdom called *Kapilavastu*, and the queen *Maya*. Although he was raised as a prince, he renounced the world at the age of 29 to seek after the truth and attained Great Enlightenment at the age of 35. After performing the first preaching at the Deer Park or *Magadaava* (the First Turning of the Wheel of Truth), he continued to preach the law throughout India until he died at the age of 80. After his death, Buddhism became a world religion. *Shakyamuni* is an abbreviation of *Shakyamuni bhagavat* (the honorary name meaning "World-Honored One of the *Shakya* clan").

1
Before Recording Shakyamuni Buddha's Future Prediction

The novel coronavirus problem has come to look like *The War of the Worlds*

RYUHO OKAWA

When I received some spiritual messages about the novel coronavirus infection early this year, the number of infected people was still in the tens of thousands and there were only around several hundred deaths. We recorded the spiritual messages when the situation was still around that level, but now in the middle of April, almost two million people around the world have been infected and over

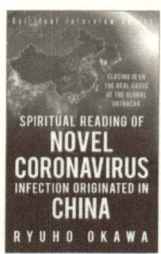

Spiritual Reading of Novel Coronavirus Infection Originated in China: Closing in on the real cause of the global outbreak (Tokyo: HS Press, 2020)

100,000 have died. In America, there have been more than half a million infected cases and more than 20,000 deaths. Countries like Spain and Italy have also suffered around 20,000 deaths. So, even advanced countries are starting to see the death toll reach tens of thousands across the board. Japan has plateaued at around several thousand infected cases, but a State of Emergency has been declared due to uncertainty over whether or not the virus will continue to spread in the future. We have been living like this for about a month now.

However, the whole situation is quite bad. We are being told not to meet others and to just stay at home. This is almost like a gamble. We would be lucky if we can get the spread under control in just a month, but if we can't, then everything may be headed toward collapse.

The government is saying that it's going to scatter cash around. If it is just to compensate for a single month, this might be doable. But if everyone ends up permanently unemployed, this will be quite difficult to continue. Businesses are being told to reduce the number of in-office workers by 70 percent. In New York, they are telling everyone to absolutely stay at home. So, I think you could say that the situation is quite serious. If you were to take a world map and color in all the places infected, you would see that the virus has almost spread throughout the world. So, the situation has come to look like *The War of the Worlds* or something like that.

We would be lucky if this were over in a month, but after hearing many different people make their predictions, they all said that the infection will spread even further. If the State of Emergency lasts for up to three months, we will begin to see a complete breakdown of employment. Something far worse than even the Great Depression might occur. In addition, the simple act of people gathering or meeting is now seen as bad or wrong, so it also seems like we are approaching the downfall of civilization.

The spirit of John Lennon said, "It's Divine Will, so it can't be helped"

RYUHO OKAWA
This morning, I spoke with the spirit of John Lennon (see Chapter Two). I had been thinking about writing a prayer

or a song or something in English that would have the power to drive away the illness, but when I spoke with John Lennon, he said, "It's Divine Will, so it can't be helped."

His conclusion was something like, "It is the will of heaven to reduce the population. The Earth's population has greatly increased and the people's worldly sense of values is turning the planet into a factory for creating hellish spirits. If the percentage of people that go to hell increases as the overall number of people does, then it makes sense to reduce the population. The only option left is to reach the state of perfect tranquility called nirvana, as preached by Shakyamuni Buddha." I don't know exactly what he meant by that usage, but it sounded like he was saying, "Go back to the other world."

He pointed out that the rampant spread of this virus and the rampant spread of humanity are nearly in sync with each other. His comments seemed to contain views and judgments as follows: humanity's existence in this world as well as their actions makes him think they are growing in number to engage only in meaningless, negative, and hellish things.

Daring to ask Shakyamuni Buddha, who chooses his words carefully, about his predictions for the future

RYUHO OKAWA

That was the suggestion from John Lennon. And while Shakyamuni Buddha may not be very fond of making future predictions, I have been asking other spirits, so I think I will ask him as well. He may refuse, though [*laughs*]. He may put an end to it by saying, "According to the Law of Cause and Effect, what you are doing will lead to your result." If he does, that will be all for his prediction. The spiritual message might be over in a minute.

Shakyamuni Buddha must observe the precept of Right Speech and speak the truth, so it will be somewhat difficult for him. He cannot speak freely as he likes, as others do.

The original Buddhist scriptures contain a story about Shakyamuni, in which a man asked him, "Would you please come to my place tomorrow to preach? I invite you and 200 of your disciples for a meal." Shakyamuni gave no reply and remained silent. The reason he didn't answer was that, if he had said yes but later become unable to go, it would have meant he lied. That shows how careful Shakyamuni is. His words will remain in some form, so I don't know what kind of words he will use today.

However, other spirits have given their opinions, so I am quite sure he will at least tell us his thinking and impressions. I would like you to explore deeper into John Lennon's words, "Enter Nirvana taught by Shakyamuni Buddha." If you ask a foolish question, he might cut the conversation short, so please be very careful when you ask questions.

[*Lightly claps once.*] I would now like to receive a spiritual message from Shakyamuni, also known as Gautama Siddhartha, Buddha, and the World-Honored One. I don't know if it will be possible, but I would appreciate it if you could focus on future predictions, meaning what will happen in the future and what we should do from now on. And if people in Japan and the world today are wrong, please point out the source of their mistakes and explain why they are wrong.

[*About 10 seconds of silence.*]

2

Now Is the Time to Think about a World Ruled by Death

"You cannot build the future as an extension of the present"

SHAKYAMUNI BUDDHA
[*Exhales.*] Yes.

A

Thank you very much for coming down to Happy Science today. As Master Ryuho Okawa just explained, the novel coronavirus that originated in China is now rampant throughout the world. The number of people infected in the world is approaching two million and 110,000 have died. In Japan, around 8,000 people have been infected and more than 100 have died. That is the current situation.

This coronavirus infection has become a pandemic and the situation is growing more and more critical. So first, I would like to ask your impressions after seeing the current state of Japan and the rest of the world. What are your views?

SHAKYAMUNI BUDDHA
The current situation might mean that you can't build the future as an extension of the present. I think the current pandemic is revealing that popular and mainstream things will come to a dead end. The question is how long people will be able to survive hiding away in their homes. The ongoing situation is like life on board a submarine, so I don't think they can survive hidden forever.

I get the feeling that the time has come for them to stop and think. If this world is too comfortable to live in, people will consider this worldly way of life to be right and be contaminated by that value system. One significant thing about this current disaster is the power to stop the values and public opinions that are rampantly spreading in the world like a virus. Things that had been approved can no longer be done. In a sense, humans are being given an opportunity to reform themselves.

Now is an age when you must consider the meaning of death

A
We have been leading up to this moment ever since the virus began spreading globally from sometime around the end of last year and the beginning of this year. What do you foresee happening to the world as we move forward?

SHAKYAMUNI BUDDHA
Hmm... It will probably become a world ruled by death. I believe you are entering an age when all of you will have to think about death. Hospitals have already reached the limit of their ability, so you will witness with your own eyes the prides of the modern age, namely medicine, science, and technology, be helplessly defeated. People will have to consider the meaning of death and will likely feel their own death close at hand.

You never know who will get pneumonia from the virus and die tomorrow. In the near future, television personalities, politicians, business leaders, and other well-known figures will die one after another. Seeing this, people will surely realize that everything is passing by. It is an undeniable fact that an age will begin in which not a single worldly power will be effective.

However, in my opinion, Buddhism began during a similar age. It was an age in which humanity felt powerless. The power of humanity has grown so large and people now feel like they can control everything. Now, all eight billion people in the world are becoming more and more conceited and prideful, like long-nosed tengu goblins. But I think the time has come for their long noses to get bent.

The virus is just a symbol. I don't think you should focus too much on the virus itself. If you look back over time, you will realize there have been many different omens predicting this crisis, including major earthquakes, massive tsunamis, volcanic explosions, and other disasters. There have been acts of terrorism and wars, and if you look farther back, there were the atomic bombings in WWII. Before that, there was the Great Depression, which was nearly 100 years ago. War was necessary to get out of the Great Depression, so powerful countries started one. I think there will be another great depression this time, so there will either be a war or this virus will deprive countries of the ability to wage war before one breaks out. It feels like you are living through such a transition period.

What if the situation in New York occurs in other places worldwide?

B

Seeing the situation as it is, Master Ryuho Okawa called some spirits to ask their opinions. For example, he summoned Dr. Shibasaburo Kitasato, the father of bacteriology in Japan, and when we asked him about his outlook, he predicted that, in the future, as many as 500 million people will die from the coronavirus. And on April 9, we called up the spirit of the early-modern American clairvoyant Edgar Cayce, the so-called Sleeping Prophet.

The Novel Coronavirus Originated in China: Lessons for Humankind: Spiritual messages from Shibasaburo Kitasato and R. A. Goal (Tokyo: HS Press, 2020)

He predicted that four billion people will get infected and that 800 million, which is roughly 20 percent of them, will die. Under the current circumstances, people around the world as well as in Japan are concerned about how much the damage will be in the future. How far will this "world ruled by death" go? We would very much appreciate it if you could teach us about these things.

SHAKYAMUNI BUDDHA
Seeing how things are occurring in places like New York, if similar conditions occur in other places worldwide, then things might end up like how Edgar Cayce predicted. New York has a population of eight million, and already, more than 100,000 people have been infected. It seems like you've already plunged into a state of war. From now on, the numbers will increase exponentially, just like the rate

What Will Become of Coronavirus Pandemic?: Readings by Edgar Cayce (Tokyo: HS Press, 2020)

that lotus flowers multiply. So, the numbers could go up considerably and I don't think it will take much time to get there.

So, it's a matter of whether or not some variable will appear to prevent that from happening. Things could change if some variable capable of halting that exponential growth were to appear, but if things continue as is, I mean, if the circumstances in New York continue to occur in other places, then that's what will happen.

How many people would be infected or die if the current conditions in Japan were the global standard?

SHAKYAMUNI BUDDHA

Now, in Japan, people don't know if declaring a state of emergency will have any effect or not. But at least, the virus does seem to be spreading slower in Japan than it is in other countries. If the world were in the same condition as Japan is in now, then the damage might not be so bad. Hmm...

I wonder. Almost two million people have been infected so far, so even if that were the case, there will still likely be more than 10 million people infected.

B
Ten million people?

SHAKYAMUNI BUDDHA
There will probably be more than 10 million people infected.

B
More?

SHAKYAMUNI BUDDHA
It won't take long for the number of infected cases to increase from two million to 10 million. Also, even advanced countries are in such a state, so when it spreads to semi-developed and developing countries, they will be powerless. Tens of millions of people will be infected at the very least. However, there is also the possibility of

great minds putting their heads together and developing some sort of a vaccine. That would be another variable. Yet another possibility is for some genius to come up with a way to stop this.

Just to let you know, a future in which everyone in the world spends all of their time staying at home may not last so long. Like the nuclear winter that people talked about several decades ago, which was the idea that humanity would have to live underground, they wouldn't be able to go outside because nuclear weapons would contaminate the entire world. Other possibilities include the Earth being hit by a massive amount of radiation from outer space or a giant meteor falling and making nearly everything on the surface of the planet perish. The situation would be similar to that. So, if the conditions in the world were like Japan, there may only be tens of millions infected and hundreds of thousands of deaths. But if the world ends up being like New York, there will be many more infected cases and deaths.

A modern witch hunt could also occur

B

As you just mentioned, Japan might be much better off in terms of infections, but according to Edgar Cayce, Japan will return to where it was at the end of WWII and we should therefore improve its system of self-sufficiency.

He even said that this pandemic will become a simulation of the last day on Earth. Can we assume that, even if some variable improves the situation, the conditions similar to a simulation of the last day on Earth will continue for some time?

SHAKYAMUNI BUDDHA

That could happen and a modern witch hunt could also occur.

B

What do you mean by a witch hunt?

SHAKYAMUNI BUDDHA

Hmm... I mean, as soon as people hear that someone is infected with the virus, he or she will be instantly quarantined. In some cases, in places like China, I cannot rule out the possibility that people could be buried, literally.

B
You mean, people will become extremely cold and harsh toward infected people as soon as they find out?

SHAKYAMUNI BUDDHA
Right. When someone tests positive right now, they receive medical treatment. People talk about the medical system breaking down, but it could get to a point where people are quarantined as soon as they are tested positive, which is similar to how the Jews were. Once the death toll crosses a certain line, you will have to cremate the dead. Infections will spread further in countries that typically bury the dead.

If that's the case, people might start cremating those infected before they even die. You might end up being forced to witness the kinds of acts you least want to see. It is quite possible that large-scale cremations will be done at places like baseball stadiums where baseball can no longer be played.

However, there may be variables in any era.

"If this world becomes more like a Utopia, the population will be allowed to grow"

A

Please allow me to confirm one thing. According to the spiritual message from John Lennon that we received earlier, Grim Reapers have now been unleashed throughout the world, and they and the Archangels share the same idea.

SHAKYAMUNI BUDDHA
[*Smiles wryly.*] Really?

A

Yes. He made it sound like it is God's intention to reduce the population. What do you think about this?

SHAKYAMUNI BUDDHA
Hmm... I don't really agree with the human population in this world continuing to increase. People's mistaken way of life in this world created hell, so if this world becomes more like a Utopia, the population will be allowed to grow. But if this world becomes more hellish, that would not be very desirable. You're currently under a state of emergency, and

at the same time, people are trying to stop doing unhealthy things. Healthy things are being excluded too, but people are also trying to eliminate unhealthy things, which may seem a bit like going back to the way things used to be. I hope that humanity is given an opportunity to move from its current insane state back to sanity.

It's a matter of what people will do when they feel that they might die over the next couple of days. Some people might even go crazy and shoot a bunch of people with a machine gun. There may be some people who take it out on others like that. But people might think about their eternal life and devote themselves to God if they think they might die in a day or two.

I think the same kind of things happened during the Kamakura period. Back then, the people faced famine, infectious diseases, and the threat of foreign invasions, and various Buddhist sects also spread throughout Japan. So, in the modern age as well, in a different form, it wouldn't be at all strange for someone to appear who tries to preach the Gospel and save people.

However, if you look at the current situation, it seems that the novel coronavirus originated in an atheistic country and is spreading quite widely in Christian countries as well as in Islamic countries. A disadvantage for those who preach religion is that large groups of people cannot gather, so in that sense, religious activities are being denied.

Will humans awaken or not? I'm not sure, but to me, it does not seem desirable for the human population in this world to grow so much.

3

Now Is the Last Chance for Humankind to Change Direction

A time of population increase is also a time when a savior's power weakens

A

I would like to ask once again about the significance of a crisis like this occurring in 2020. A spirit told us that the virus began to spread just before China attempted to cause a conflict with the purpose of invading another country and that although 2020 is said to mark the beginning of a Golden Age, it will not at all be an easy period; it is also the beginning of an age of suffering and sadness. Could you please tell us about the significance of the age beginning in 2020 from your point of view?

SHAKYAMUNI BUDDHA

A time of population increase is also a time when a savior's power is weakened. It is a time when common people want to become gods in a negative sense. So, it includes such difficulties.

You are living in an age when it is difficult to tell whether or not the things that spread and become popular in society are truly imbued with the Light of God. After some time, what becomes extremely popular in Japan as well as the world might turn out to be vulgar. Things that are truly important sometimes do not spread.

I believe there are three kinds of people: those who can only realize something after it happens, those who realize it as it is happening, and those who realize it before it happens. But at this time, I can't help but say I'm disappointed.

Humankind still has some time to think

B
During the spiritual message from John Lennon earlier, he mentioned that this is inevitable because people have forgotten about God and that we should have Buddha exterminate humankind once and for all.

SHAKYAMUNI BUDDHA

I won't do that. [*Bitter smile.*] I won't exterminate you.

B

But John Lennon strongly emphasized that atheistic hedonism will not be forgiven and that there's no need for people who do not obey God.

Also, according to the explanations and teachings you gave earlier, all eight billion people in the world are becoming more and more conceited and prideful, like long-nosed tengu goblins, and now is a time when people want to become gods. In other words, people are now living a worldly way of life. Are these phenomena occurring because atheistic hedonism and a worldly way of life will not be forgiven? Is this will working behind the scenes? Or, are people getting what they deserve, in other words, are their own evil thoughts attracting these things? We would very much appreciate it if you could teach us what is going on behind the scenes spiritually.

SHAKYAMUNI BUDDHA

It is as you imagine. But humankind is lucky to have been given the time to think at all.

If a 10-km-wide meteor were detected on a collision course with the Earth and couldn't be avoided at all, there would be nothing you could do but to wait for it to hit.

But while this virus is spreading, you still have some time to think. As it continues to spread, you will surely realize how frail modern civilization is, so you might end up having to think up a new form of civilization.

It's about human survival. Only a few people are predicting that humans will be totally destroyed. So, basically, if humankind is able to survive, the civilization that survives will take on a slightly different form. I'm sure different things will be common and popular from those right now. A lot of things could set it off. That's what would happen in the case of a meteor strike. Hmm... Many options have been prepared and thought up.

B
Like earthquakes, rise in the sea level, volcanic eruptions, and so on...

SHAKYAMUNI BUDDHA
Yes, such kinds of things, too. There might also be illnesses different from the one caused by the coronavirus. Take the

propagation of locusts as an example. If they were to cover the entire Earth, that would be the end. All that would be left of humans and animals would be bones. You might not know why things like that happen, but you mentioned some sort of will at work, and I think you are exactly right. But there is still some time to think, and still time to convey this will to change things. I think this is fortunate.

B
I see...

Preach how human beings should be and fight to prevent a future controlled by AI

C
Right now, even atheists are being challenged as to what they can realize when faced with death. At the same time, though, believers of Christianity and Islam also find themselves in severe circumstances where they cannot satisfactorily pray and congregate. So, even for people who have been believers in existing religions, I think now is the

time for them to realize something. What do you think these believers in existing religions should realize?

SHAKYAMUNI BUDDHA
Just one thing. They just need to realize that humans are not supreme. It is important for them to accept that there is a being above them who teaches which direction they should go in.

If the situation continues as it is, then in the future, humankind will think that a computer-based society or AI is a god instead of thinking that humans are supreme. At this rate, it will happen very soon. As I said earlier, in the future, there will be a time when AI will look at the spread of infections and make decisions like, "It would be better to eliminate the residents of this area."

However, I do feel that the trend at work is something that is trying to change the course of this civilization, which is heading toward deifying AI. To be honest, though, many of the work that Happy Science does can't be done by AI. But competing against you, the trend to move from computers to AI will spread faster… In today's world, you can connect the entire world together like a network, through which you can spread that trend, pollution, or destruction.

Japan might be behind the times, but if an order to reduce office attendance by 70 percent is issued, you can immediately calculate the number of people who will be crossing crosswalks and riding trains, right? Which means that you are already living in a society where everything is controlled. What awaits in the future for humankind without God is an AI-controlled future. And if nothing changes the current course, AI will become a god. Maybe after 2050. It may happen before that.

However, I also think there needs to appear something that opposes this. In particular, if people continue to get infected and die, it will mean that, in the future, more and more things will operate according to the decisions made by AI, in many fields such as politics, government administration, and commerce. Instead of people hiding away in their homes, AI might decide everything about how the world runs. There may come a time when AI will determine how resources are distributed, how trade is implemented, and how much is consumed.

In response, you, Happy Science, are returning to the essence of what it means to be human and preaching how human beings should be. This is a frustrating style. The number of people you can preach to at one time is very limited. Be that as it may, though, you are the last stand. God will not approve of this (AI-controlled) future.

If humans don't notice now, something worse might come

B
So, you mean that the current situation caused by the novel coronavirus is forcing us to choose what kind of a new civilization we want to build?

SHAKYAMUNI BUDDHA
Events like continents sinking into the sea will be awaiting you in the future. You will be looking at the commonly conceivable, usual process of death in which people get infected by the virus, develop pneumonia, and die. But if this is not enough for people to notice, then continents really will sink into the sea.

In the past, there have been several instances of entire civilizations disappearing. And it won't happen as slowly as you imagine. It doesn't happen slowly over hundreds of millions of years as modern geophysics says. It happens quite frequently, in a cycle of about 10,000 years. For example, if the country of Japan is judged to be harmful to humankind enough to be destroyed, it's possible to make it sink into the sea. Of course, it's possible to raise the sea level to cover it up, or to blanket it in volcanic ash. Or, we can make Japan the North Pole in order to bury it under a field of ice. Everything is possible. There are many ways to do it.

Things like that are lying in wait. So, people get brought to the hospital as they fall sick and they receive treatment. But there will be many who will not have access to treatment and will die. During this period, you should revise the nature of the current civilization, otherwise you will face something even larger in scale next.

I'm not the only one saying this. Again and again, people mention that there have been past civilizations, but no one seems to listen to it seriously. You must ask yourself, "If there were civilizations in the past, why are there no traces of them now?" You have to realize the reason why. What's coming in the future could be even more devastating. Now is the Golden Age because humankind is being given an opportunity to change direction. In other words, now is your last chance.

B
I see.

4

Why Is the Virus Spreading?

The virus symbolizes all of humankind

B

We are facing the process of death resulting from the novel coronavirus. However, we still have time to realize what the problem is and change the way we think. Therefore, although the current situation looks grim, we have more of a chance than if we were to all die instantly in a sudden meteor strike. Is that what you mean?

SHAKYAMUNI BUDDHA

Right. Humans may feel alive and healthy, but if infected by a virus, they will get sick and feel unwell. People can understand this. However, they completely fail to understand the idea of not being able to return to the Real World as a result of their heart or soul becoming tainted and corrupt. It's because they live in rejection of this understanding. Therein lies a mistake, and we want to change this.

The virus is symbolic. It symbolizes all of humanity. The human population has been increasing at a rapid pace and covers the surface of the Earth like a virus. When Happy Science was founded, there were five billion people in the world. Now, it's between seven and eight billion. I'm sure it's only a matter of time before you reach 10 billion. There will surely be that many people by the year 2050. Humanity has now been presented with a major question: "Is it OK to continue as-is, knowing that there will be 10 billion people by 2050?"

There are many different levels of unhappiness, but the kind of unhappiness that stops people in their tracks, makes them turn around and rethink things is the kind of unhappiness that leads people onto the right path. Many people are going to die. People are born, they age, fall sick, and die. Death can come from an epidemic, war, starvation, pollution, and many other causes. But from the Buddhist perspective, all of these occur so that you will think about the meaning of death, realize that you are all equal under death, and eventually accept your own mortality. It's only a matter of whether it happens sooner rather than later. People will either accept this simple enlightenment about the meaning of this world, or not. Once they have accepted this simple enlightenment on the principle of life, it becomes a matter of whether or not they come to have faith in Him who leads humanity. That's what it depends on. If this way of thinking is able to spread faster than the pace at which the virus is, then the world will change, and everyone possesses the potential to do this.

However, although both the mass media and minor media outlets accessible by individuals spread information throughout the world, unfortunately, their contents do not convey these Truths. Users are following materialistic content most of the time.

Whether this becomes a true Golden Age or not depends on how you practice the law of cause and effect. It depends on what sorts of causal acts you perform and on what effects those have. Happy Science has now been active for more than 30 years. But Japanese society has also been working hard to categorize you as just one of many religions. They ridicule you because they mistakenly believe that the activities you are doing to save the world are instead motivated by the desire for fame, power, status, goods, and wealth. The time will come for them to pay the price.

It depends on whether or not Japan itself can acquire enough power to save the world

B

A moment ago, you said that the situation may change slightly if there were a variable of some sort. You also taught us that, if humankind wakes up to the Truth and has faith in things like Buddha's Truth, Divine Light, and the existence of God and Buddha, then the future of the Earth could change. A space being named R. A. Goal also said that, if we maintain faith in the face of negative thoughts and malignant viruses, it will develop into "faith immunity," or "faith vaccine," and we will not die. Are there any important points that would help us come to the realizations that we require in order to possess faith vaccine while still living in modern society where materialistic values have spread?

SHAKYAMUNI BUDDHA

At any rate, if you look at the world, you can see that most of the so-called Western countries are powerful Christian nations. On the exact opposite side, atheistic and materialistic countries centered on gigantic China are growing. In the lands between these live Muslims, who engage in guerrilla-style warfare and who are regarded as a problem. How should they be evaluated? And it can already be predicted that, if Japan continues to do nothing amidst this situation, then, in the blink of an eye, Japan could drop from its position as no.3 in the world down to no. 20 or lower. Seeing this, nothing originating from Japan would be able to dominate the world. Japan will probably have no choice but to ally with one side or the other. Japan is trying to survive by focusing only on the good points of both sides. It's a matter of whether Japan itself can acquire enough power to save the world, or at the very least, a matter of whether or not something originating from Japan can proliferate as a way of reforming or converting the world. There is still a chance of something like that. And regardless of how successful that is, future society will likely develop from within it.

Cross-cultural contact causes epidemics

B

In terms of Japan's history and its profound belief in gods, as recorded in the *Kojiki* and *Nihon Shoki*, which are ancient Japanese documents, it's said that Japanese Shinto has been practiced for the last 2,700 years.

Recently, a being named Kuni-no-Tokotachi-no-Kami* negotiated several times with Master Ryuho Okawa because he very much wished to speak. He is one of the many gods in Japan, and when we spoke with him, he asserted that Japan doesn't need foreign gods and that the virus is spreading because foreign gods have come to Japan.

I hope that something originating from Japan will have a major, positive impact, but at the same time, for the sake of their own ego and to make themselves look good, some of these ancient deities are denying all of the foreign gods that have come to Japan. And some are saying things like, "The virus is spreading because faith in El Cantare has grown." If, from your point of view, you have any judgments on

---
* Refer to the spiritual recording, "Readings by Kuni-no-Tokotachi-no-Kami and Edgar Cayce: What Will Become of Coronavirus Pandemic?," available at all Happy Science locations.

Kuni-no-Tokotachi-no-Kami's assertion, such as about how one of the gods that are connected with the rear side of the Spirit World is impeding Japan's innovativeness and future, or other related conditions in the Spirit World, could you please teach us about them?

SHAKYAMUNI BUDDHA
Well, in a worldly sense, I think that some of what he says is accurate. During the period when Buddhism was introduced into Japan, foreign products of culture came with people to the country. At the same time, unknown pathogens were also entering Japan. As a result, diseases to which Japanese people had no immunity prevailed. All kinds of epidemics spread in Japan.

It was during the reign of Prince Shotoku. That's why opposing forces appeared from within Japanese Shinto, claiming that the epidemics occurred because Buddhism was allowed into the country. It wasn't just statues of Buddha that entered. As foreign people, foreign food, and a variety of other things entered this country, viruses sometimes entered along with them, which caused diseases to spread. That sort of thing happened.

Also, before the Meiji period, ever since Commodore Perry's arrival, Japan was already westernizing as a result of foreign visitors, and by stepping foot in Edo, now Tokyo, these foreigners caused a massive outbreak of cholera. Cholera flourished from the Meiji period all the way through to the Taisho period. That was a direct result of foreigners coming into the country. It appears that cholera was introduced hand-in-hand with Christianity. This sort of cross-cultural contact introduces positive aspects, but sometimes it can have negative results as well.

Now, the world is connected through trade and transportation, which is why this virus originating from China is spreading to the ends of the world. The coronavirus has made it all the way to Argentina, New Zealand, and Norway, which in the past would have been unthinkable. This has happened precisely due to the nature of the modern age. This sort of thing is possible.

So, in a worldly sense, I think that some of what that god said is accurate. By introducing new things, there occurred contamination and epidemics that otherwise would not have entered an isolated island nation.

Going by the ancient interpretation, this is the result of believing in foreign gods, but actually, it was due to foreigners coming into the country. I believe that it is due to the influx of foreign citizens and their products of culture.

If this sort of outbreak had happened back when the only contact with China was the ships taken by Japanese envoys to the Tang dynasty, then all you would need to do would have been to stop sending those ships in order to keep the Chinese virus out of the country. That would completely block the virus.

It depends on whether or not you can spread Buddha's Truth wider and faster and turn it into a trend

SHAKYAMUNI BUDDHA
But in the current situation, the flow of traffic wasn't stopped, and a huge number of people flew in on airplanes. Then, via Japan, the virus spread to the rest of the world. That's how it happened.

Shakyamuni Buddha's Future Prediction

The entire world is interconnected, and this gives these sorts of highly contagious diseases the ability to destroy the world. Even diseases that only exist on a single island nation or among a single, particular, minor ethnicity could spread throughout the world.

Columbus brought syphilis back to Europe from the West Indies, a series of islands in the Caribbean Sea, and within 100 years, the disease spread throughout the entire world. In the modern age, diseases that would have taken 100 years to spread in the past are now able to spread within a single year.

But if bad things can spread, good things must spread as well. It depends on whether you can turn into trends the idea that good things must spread. They work in the same way. That's also what you disciples are fighting to do. You use the word *spread* to describe the virus going rampant, in the same way you use it to say, "Let's spread Buddha's Truth."

Viruses spread rapidly. But Happy Science teachings haven't spread very far. You publish books, give lectures, and even make movies and music, but they still aren't spreading as rapidly as the virus. I guess that's the fight, though.

Shakyamuni Buddha's Future Prediction

Like Saint Nichiren, you need to have the passion to continue preaching even if people are throwing stones at you, and at the same time, you need to think about whether or not you are quick and wide enough to deal with your enemies outside the group in the modern age.

5

What Is Required of Us Now

Thinking about "what is required of us now" from the perspective of future generations

C

You suggested that the current activities carried out by Happy Science members will determine the future trends and the course of civilization. In order to further spread the teachings, we require even stronger resolve. I believe that the disciples who have gathered at Happy Science should continue to engage in salvation work while being glad to bear responsibility for the future of humanity. I would appreciate it if you could teach us the Right Will we should develop as we proceed.

SHAKYAMUNI BUDDHA

Hmm… Overall, Happy Science seems to operate like a company. If it does, the influence of your work is determined by the scale of the organization. Since there are many companies in Japan and throughout the world that are much larger in scale than your organization, your level of influence and power wouldn't even be on par with a single one of those major companies. So, you need to spread religiously, not just in terms of the corporate structure.

If your teachings won't spread unless you turn the entire world into "public servants" employed by Happy Science and have them work all over the world, you will never get very far.

Right now, if someone like the prime minister or a prefectural governor of Japan issues a state of emergency, they can order people not to go to work, and instead tell them to stay at home, refrain from shopping for nonessential items, and so on. It's similar to life during a war, and those messages are gradually pervading society to some extent. Unfortunately, though, the Words of God don't seem to spread enough in the same way.

This is symbolized by the fact that, it is of course difficult to convey the Truth, both overseas and in Japan, and political activities are also difficult. There is also the fact that the media outlets that have been infected by the materialistic "communism virus" are the ones that are powerful.

It's going to be a fight. Unfortunately, though, I feel that each one of you disciples might be too weak. The disciples as well might be "tainted" by modern education and culture. They are at the level of not becoming aware of what their mission is unless a huge number of people actually get infected and die, being forced to live in the depths of despair. You look like you're just continuously focused on achieving the small goals you have set for yourselves. So, I feel that you yourselves are already caught in the quicksand that is the modern civilization. Please think deeply about what is required of you now, from the perspective of future generations. Because that is very important.

If you were to conduct a democratic vote or a survey among the citizens of Japan and ask them, "Do you believe in the other world? Yes or no?" I am sure most people would vote "no." This is how Japanese democracy is able to deny the existence of God. They are also able to deny the existence of the other world and spirits. The ones that are happy about this are the devils in hell because they are able to spread the idea that there is no next world and that people should act freely because this world is all there is. Devils are also happy to see worldly values become one with the values of the other world.

At first glance, it may seem like unhappiness is now prevailing, but I believe that it is at times like this that people are being tested to see whether or not they are able to work hard enough to reverse the downward trend and spread spiritual values.

One factor behind the spread of coronavirus infections is humanity's self-punishment

A

A moment ago, Mr. B mentioned Kuni-no-Tokotachi-no-Kami, who is furious at the modern atheistic and materialistic world and one of his assertions is that faith in gods is necessary. What he meant, though, was faith in ancient Japanese gods. World religions like Christianity and Islam also probably preach the necessity of faith in existing gods. But we want to spread faith in El Cantare[*] throughout the world. We would appreciate it if you could once again give us a comment about the type of faith that will be necessary in the future.

---

[*] The Supreme God of the Earth Spirit Group; God of the Earth who has guided humanity since the beginning of Earth and who was also involved in the Creation of the universe. Today, El Cantare has descended on Earth as Master Ryuho Okawa. See the end section, and also Ryuho Okawa, *The Laws of the Sun* and *The Laws of Faith* (both New York: IRH Press, 2018).

SHAKYAMUNI BUDDHA

[*About five seconds of silence.*] People have been forbidden to go to work or school, so in a sense, right now, people have nothing to do. Many people might not have had the chance to consider things like these unless they had a bit of leisure time or some mental space. They fill their head with information learned in school and think that if they get into a good university, they will find a good job, and then they will have "won" in life in this world. Or, they think that they should just take a higher position in their company, make money, or any number of other things. If people focus on the negative aspects of this situation, they will find a lot of negative things. However, on the bright side, they now have a chance to think.

Some people think that this infection is a divine punishment, and I think that's somewhat true, but it is humanity's self-punishment in the first place. There will be some reaction from people deceiving and betraying themselves. If people can't understand that, though it may be too difficult to return to a primitive lifestyle, it might be a good idea for them to restart their lives just as they did when they were defeated in WWII.

If, from now on, even Christian countries experience an infection surge and a large number of deaths which far exceed anything seen in war, then that will shake people's faith. It's the same with Islamic nations. For example, if Muslims gather in a dome to pray to Allah, but get infected while they are there, it would mean Allah is completely powerless.

I think the current battle is also about whether or not faith in God will completely surrender to materialism. Hospitals have become "shrines" and doctors have become "gods," right? The ideas, "hospitals as Shinto shrines and Buddhist temples" and "doctors serving as Shinto or Buddhist priests" are reaching their limits. In the coming generations, once the space age begins, something similar will probably happen again as the previously unknown come to the Earth from outer space.

What you need to show people right now is the power of faith. What can be accomplished through faith? What exactly will the power of faith prove? What does it mean to have faith in God? What human potential will be unlocked once they realize their original, true self?

When you pray to the True God, you will know the True God

SHAKYAMUNI BUDDHA

Most people are given lives of no more than 100 years. But when illnesses like this spread, you can't tell how long you will be able to live.

The other day, British Prime Minister Johnson was suddenly hospitalized and put in the ICU. His soul left his body and came to Mr. Ryuho Okawa to be saved.* The meeting was very brief, but he received light and returned to his body. He has since been discharged from the hospital and is currently undergoing rehabilitation. When he prayed to God, he ended up coming here. I don't think that was his guardian spirit. It was probably the spirit of Johnson, himself. I think it left his body and came here. He is now on his way to recovery. When you pray to the True God, in some cases, you will know the True God. He (Ryuho Okawa) was supposed to leave for England soon in order to spread the Gospel among the people there, but was unable

---
* See *Jesus Christ's Answers to the Coronavirus Pandemic* (Tokyo: HS Press, 2020)

to go under this circumstance.* How can anyone give a lecture when the people there may be fined if they hold a gathering of three or more people? That's an artificial measure, but when the leader of that country showed strong faith in God, he came all the way to El Cantare. German Prime Minister Merkel is also Christian, and she is obviously praying to God. That's why she came to El Cantare.

Will people eventually realize that there exists a being far above the Christian God, instead of deifying Jesus? Will people understand that there is a being that surpasses Allah, the Islamic God recognized by Muhammad? Religion, too, will experience this kind of battle.

There are many temples and shrines in Japan, and they enshrine *honzon*, or objects of worship, but there exists something beyond them. The issue is whether or not people can reach that level of recognition.

---

* The author was originally scheduled to give a lecture in Spring 2020 in London, U.K., but it was then canceled after the British government ordered a lockdown to prevent people from going out or gathering in groups.

You must realize that not knowing yourself is a sin

SHAKYAMUNI BUDDHA
If those responsible for managing temples and shrines received a materialistic education at Japanese universities, they could not work miracles at all. If they feel that they can't go on like this, they will just begin to offer prayers that go beyond materialism. There is still a chance, though. That's why I think it is important to teach people about the existence of this way of thinking. Basically, divine punishment does exist, but it is also self-punishment. Not knowing yourself is a sin. Knowing that you have a physical body but not knowing that your soul dwells within it while going through spiritual training, is a sin. It is like knowing there is a car but not knowing there is a driver. You might assume you are driving a self-driving car, but no, there is a driver. It is, after all, a sin to lose sight of yourself. You have to realize this. Self-discovery leads to the discovery of God.

B
So, in other words, the extent to which a person is able to discover themselves is a spiritual challenge each one of

us must take on, and this self-discovery will show human beings the path to the next civilization and also provide them the path to salvation. Did I understand you correctly?

SHAKYAMUNI BUDDHA

An age of despair is also an age when religions make a breakthrough. But we are not trying to "prey" on unhappiness. Rather, when faced with a hurdle that cannot be overcome using wisdom produced by humans, you have to say, "Look for something beyond human wisdom."

6

Future Developments in International Affairs and Japan's Mission

The Great East Japan Earthquake toppled the DPJ-led administration

A

I would like to ask another question because I think it might be useful to other countries around the world. In 2011, the Great East Japan Earthquake occurred. Amaterasu-O-Mikami (the Sun Goddess) warned us about it in her spiritual message the previous year, and one of the causes seems to have been the political corruption under the DPJ (Democratic Party of Japan)-led administration at the time. The earthquake and tsunami claimed nearly 20,000 lives. However, this unfortunately did not result in many people waking up to religious faith. People's values did not change. How, then, should we perceive major catastrophes that result in numerous victims and spread faith in God, or change people's values? We would appreciate it if you could give us some advice about this sort of thing, using that Japanese disaster as a lesson.

SHAKYAMUNI BUDDHA
In regard to the Great East Japan Earthquake, it ultimately toppled the DPJ–led administration, right? Their approval rate gradually fell after that and never recovered. People saw that the administration had no ability to govern and felt that they were not blessed by God. It seemed that even the heartless mass media were feeling that way. If the country had continued to succeed under the DPJ-led administration, Japan would probably have become even closer to China. I think that would have resulted in China ambitiously aiming for Japan, just as they are now trying to take Taiwan.

Japan should have political, economic, and diplomatic systems that are independent of China

SHAKYAMUNI BUDDHA
That was the first attempt to separate Japan from China.

The current coronavirus pandemic will be the second attempt. So, I think the current situation has indicated that Japan needs to ensure its economy does not depend too much on China.

Furthermore, although Japan may not yet be aware of it, Japan is responsible for the current pandemic. (At the time) Japan did not deny entry to people from China. They checked passengers only from Hubei Provence and overlooked those from other parts of China, so many Chinese people fled to locations all around the world via Japan. This is what caused infections to spread throughout the world.

There may still be only a few infections in Japan, which means Chinese people just traveled to other countries by way of Japan. This resulted in the virus spreading in those countries. In that sense, people need to realize that Japan bears a considerable portion of the responsibility for the nearly two million infections in the world right now.

Therefore, when you look at these two incidents, you could say that, while it may not be possible for Japan to completely break off relations with China, they need to have their own independent political, economic, and diplomatic systems. This is because China is no longer the once-great Buddhist nation. They are now an atheistic and materialistic country. So, if Japan is a country that believes in God, they need to maintain a certain distance from such a country. You should see this as divine revelation.

China will suffer repercussions for causing this global viral outbreak

A
I have another question. China is accelerating their military operations even amid the global crisis, which originated in their own country. In addition to economic issues, do you have any advice regarding military affairs?

SHAKYAMUNI BUDDHA
It probably looks like China has overcome the worst part of the coronavirus pandemic and will get it under control soon, but in our world (the Spirit World), it is already being predicted that some new assault on China will occur. A country responsible for a global viral outbreak, which is a "cause," surely won't be able to rise up to the world leader because that is against the law of cause

and effect. So, you should believe that China will suffer repercussions accordingly.

Therefore, setting that aside, though, it is important to walk the path of righteousness. We think China will suffer major damage in the near future. They will likely suffer the second and third waves of catastrophes. But the goal of these is to completely convert China, one of the leading nations in the world and the center of materialism and atheism, into a nation that takes the Will of God to heart. That's why, now is the Golden Age.

Shakyamuni's views on the possibility of a U.S.-China war over coronavirus infections

B

If investigations by various countries around the world find out that this viral outbreak was caused by a Chinese biological weapon, then according to the spirit of Edgar Cayce, the U.S. might make war against China. What will happen in the world after it becomes clear that China is responsible for these viral infections?

SHAKYAMUNI BUDDHA

Iraqis hijacked some U.S. aircraft... Actually, they weren't Iraqis; they were Saudi Arabians who had been brainwashed by Islamic terrorists. The aircraft were hijacked by Saudi Arabian citizens and flown into the two World Trade Centers and the Pentagon, killing more than 3,000 people. This incident is now known as 9/11, and two years later, the U.S. went so far as to destroy Iraq. This was because 3,000 U.S. citizens had been killed.

In other words, while the perpetrators were citizens of Saudi Arabia, a country on friendly terms with the U.S., Americans invaded Iraq because they thought the perpetrators were acting under the influence of brainwashing by Islamic fundamentalism. That's how the U.S. is.

So far, there have been around or more than 20,000 deaths.[*] If this number is predicted to increase even further in the future, then hundreds of thousands, or even millions, of Americans will die. And if the cause is proven to be a viral weapon from a virology research institute in

---

[*] As of this recording on April 14, 2020, the number of American deaths due to the novel coronavirus infection was 29,825. One week later, on April 21, it went up to 45,318. About 90 percent of it is the number since April.

Wuhan, China, as they say, then... I don't know. It looks like they are about to get to the truth, and we are waiting on verification and evidence.

The World Health Organization (WHO) leans pro-China, so President Trump is saying he will no longer fund them. I think they intend to begin verification after expelling the WHO.

If they can prove that tens of thousands of Americans were killed by a viral weapon, or if they are able to obtain some crucial evidence, the U.S. wouldn't just let China do as they want. China will likely suffer a storm of missiles.

Japan should create a national defense system that enables it to defend itself

C
When it comes to the U.S. and China, Japan continues to take no action whatsoever even though it is located right next to China. Actually, though, I think Japan, also, has a mission as a leading nation to protect freedom in Asia. What do you think of Japan's true mission?

SHAKYAMUNI BUDDHA

Hmm... At the very least, it is clear that China has aggressive intent. If you cannot protect mutual peace diplomatically from a country with aggressive intent, you have to choose between resigning yourself to destruction and creating a national system capable of self-protection.

In Japan, the idea of ensuring that the country is able to defend itself by expanding its military capabilities was advocated by people like Shozan Sakuma. Over the last 10 years or so, the Happiness Realization Party (HRP) has also seemed to be talking about this approach, which means that the group of spirits that support the party probably agree to the idea. I am sure that the party's approach is just about never allowing other countries to occupy or destroy Japan one-sidedly.

If you possessed the power to completely disarm China, like in the situation similar to what happened to the former Japanese Empire, that would be another option. Of course, that would be a major undertaking. And China wouldn't accept it easily. Probably because, to them, it would mean their country being divided up by foreign countries again, like it was during the Qing dynasty.

I believe it is necessary to have China reduce its military capabilities, but Japan should also possess appropriate national defense capabilities. It is possible that Japan could be left defenseless if the Japan-U.S. alliance is severed with Japan still lacking its own defensive capabilities.

These were points made by the HRP at the time of its founding, and now, 11 years later, the party's continued survival depends on whether or not it can achieve those. Objectively, the party appears to be failing in a success-or-failure assessment. So, it is important for the party to show the world the reason the party exists and clearly express its opinions.

Japan's prerequisites for expressing opinions about the religious conflicts in the world

B
You just mentioned the U.S. and China as well as Japan's mission, but another major factor we can't avoid as we continue to observe the future of the world moving forward is the Middle East.

Recently, many prime ministers, heads of state, or sovereigns (either the spirits of themselves or their guardian spirits) have been visiting Master Ryuho Okawa, expecting to be saved. The spirit of British Prime Minister Johnson, whom you mentioned earlier, as well as the guardian spirits of German Chancellor Merkel and Japanese Prime Minister Abe, have all come to ask for help.

Another spirit who came to Master Ryuho Okawa to seek for help was the guardian spirit of Ayatollah Khamenei of Iran. Right now, there are more than one billion Muslims in the world, so in terms of numbers, they are closing in on Christianity.

So, if you have any guidance for the Muslims around the world, please teach us.

SHAKYAMUNI BUDDHA

This is another major issue. Islam and Christianity have been on bad terms with each other since the Crusades. The problem hasn't been settled. There are around two billion Christians and more than one billion Muslims who are "rivals" with each other, and it is said that the Muslim population will soon surpass the Christian population.

In the same way that national GDP rankings fluctuate, Muslims are about to outnumber Christians. But I don't think Christian nations will be able to stay quiet about this.

If Muslim countries become more affluent and militarily powerful, the Christian nations could possibly be destroyed. And as a prelude to this, the issue of whether Israel, the country of the Old Testament, will be destroyed or not will also likely come up. So, no matter where you are in the world, it will undoubtedly be like living next to a powder magazine.

However, you have revealed that both Christianity and Islam are connected to the Original God (Lord El Cantare) in Happy Science, and you have been telling the believers of the two religions that, even though they worship in different ways, they should strive to mutually understand each other. However, it is still unclear whether or not this message will get through to them.

So, as I mentioned earlier, Japan's activities are currently centered on the Japan-U.S. alliance, but if that alliance were to be severed due to Japan taking sides with the Islamic world, it would create an extremely unstable environment for Japan. That's why I am saying that Japan should create its own national defense system.

The U.S. has inherited the European DNA of the Crusades, but the U.S. has yet to start its own version of the Crusades, unless you see the Iraqi War or the Gulf War that way. There could one day be a U.S. president that earnestly tries to destroy Islam. For Japan to be able to express its opinions at times like that, the country must be independent. It may not be possible to get along well with every country.

At any rate, though, people in both the Christian and Islamic countries are seeking for help from Japan, and I believe the people in Taiwan, Hong Kong, and probably in places like Malaysia and Singapore are as well. There will be people asking for help from Japan, even in these areas within the so-called Greater China. So, I think it is necessary for Japan to have the "centripetal force," judgment ability, and the energy to take action required to handle that.

7

The Spiritual Backgrounds behind World Religions and Their Problems

The guidance from Elohim and Hermes lay at the root of the establishment of Islam

B

There is one more thing I would very much like to ask you. The guardian spirit of Ayatollah Khamenei visited Master Ryuho Okawa on April 12.[*] He said that he did not understand the Will of Allah, and wondered what Allah is thinking. That led to us recording a spiritual message from Allah. Surprisingly, when Master summoned the spiritual being Allah, the one who appeared was Hermes, who is one of El Cantare's branch spirits born 4,300 years ago in Greece, which showed that Allah is connected with Hermes after all.

---

[*] Refer to the spiritual recording, "Iran's Decision and Allah's True Thoughts: Spiritual Messages from the Guardian Spirit of Ayatollah Khamenei and Allah." The lecture is available at Happy Science temples, shojas, and missionary centers worldwide.

If you have any comments on this from your point of view, we would appreciate your suggestions and teachings.

SHAKYAMUNI BUDDHA
Christianity was inherited by the Roman Empire and somewhat flourished. However, it was showing signs of decline when Islam appeared. When the Great Roman Empire showed indications of decline and was approaching its end, Islam appeared as a way of ushering in the next civilization. I believe so.

At that point, Christian civilization wasn't very prominent in Europe other than in Rome, and Roman civilization had destroyed Greek civilization. Roman civilization developed by destroying Greek civilization. And I believe Islamic civilization had quite a powerful influence during the Middle Ages. It had been a major force for more than 1,000 years.

In recent years, Christianity has regained influence, particularly because the U.K. and the U.S. emerged as powerful nations again after successfully modernizing and industrializing their countries as well as due to Protestant Christianity gaining power.

In that sense, it is a fact that, after the fall of the Greek gods, Hermes guided Muhammad when he was fighting the Meccan tribes in the Islamic world. Before that, Hermes was in Greece working to unify Europe. Greece was destroyed by Rome, and then when Rome started to decline, Hermes moved to the Middle East, where he started to preach a new teaching.

In the Middle East, old religions were perishing, and with the expansion of Christianity, Manichaeism was... Actually, though, it was Zoroastrianism that destroyed Manichaeism. Zoroastrianism has now become a very tiny religion. When it was no longer a threat to Christianity, there established a religion called Manichaeism, which had a certain mission, but this too was defeated.

At one point during the third century, Manichaeism seemed likely to develop into a world religion, but actually, the reason it was founded was because of the situation Christianity was facing. Jesus was sent down to Earth in the first century AD. However, he was crucified in Israel, and Christianity was being oppressed by the Roman Empire. Christians were all being fed to lions, crucified upside down, or stoned to death. Since this continued for more than 300 years, Mani was sent down to work to create Manichaeism, but it too was destroyed.

Therefore, next, Islam was founded centering on Muhammad and those with him. I doubt that you have studied it in detail, but in the revelations from Allah, Allah's guidance within Islam included even detailed battle orders and strategies to help Muhammad in the fight against the Meccan tribes. Hermes is the only one capable of that.

So, I believe Hermes provided practical guidance, and as a larger being, Elohim* made the Middle East prosper using the great Light of Compassion.

Now is the age when a third power must develop

B

You mean, in terms of spiritual guidance, Elohim was the pillar, and Hermes provided specific instructions? Islamic

---

* One of the core consciousnesses of El Cantare, the Supreme God of the Earth Spirit Group. Elohim was born about 150 million years ago, near the area that is now the Middle East, and taught teachings of wisdom, mainly on the differences of light and darkness, and good and evil. Elohim is the same being as Allah in Islam. See *The Laws of Faith* (New York: IRH Press, 2018).

civilization was powerful, particularly when it came to commerce and military affairs. Is it OK to understand that the rise and fall of these civilizations were what El Cantare conceived of in His mind as His plan for the world?

SHAKYAMUNI BUDDHA

Happy Science is probably taking the reconstruction and development of the Middle East and Africa into consideration. I believe you have the latitude and capacity for that. The scope of your mission encompasses that. Of course, if the West continues to develop at the same rate, Islam will trail behind and never catch up with white people and Christian culture. However, it seems that the brakes are being applied to their progress. In the modern age, both sides are butting up against materialistic forces and reaching their limit. So, I also believe now is the age when a third power must develop.

Points to reflect on in modern Christianity and Islam

A

Right now, coronavirus infections are extremely rampant in Christian countries, like the U.S., Italy, Spain, and the U.K. What is the spiritual background behind this?

SHAKYAMUNI BUDDHA

People must realize the mistake in modern Christianity. Christianity is the religion of people who didn't believe in Jesus. It is a religion of people who, after crucifying Jesus themselves, claim to believe that Jesus atoned for their sins, so there is a mistake in its way of thinking. In other words, although they need to repent for persecuting and executing Jesus, they don't.

In that regard, it is the same as Judaism, the religion that killed Jesus. The reason that Christianity is able to cooperate with Judaism is that Christianity hasn't repented. They express no repentance over killing the Savior, no repentance over the Roman Empire feeding Christians to ferocious beasts, and no repentance over the crucifixion.

There has been no reflection on things like burning to death people trying to enact religious reform in witch hunts. I believe that Christianity is now in need of reform because of the lack of such repentance. Also, the corruption within the Vatican seems quite severe to me as well. Countries like Italy, Spain, and Portugal are, after all, responsible for going all the way to Central and South America to conduct missionary work, so I think they probably bear a certain amount of negative karma. The downfall and duplicity of Latin Catholicism seem especially severe. India has also become a multi-religious country, and it now requires some sort of religious modernization.

A
Coronavirus infections are spreading in the Middle East as well, mainly in Iran. Does this also have a spiritual background?

SHAKYAMUNI BUDDHA
Hmm, it might mean that they are not completely innocent. There may be some kind of a problem. It might mean that Allah loving all people equally is not

the same as forcing everyone to be equally poor. People there are struggling economically, right? Life is hard for a huge number of people there, so even though religious leaders are running the country, things aren't going well. I think this means it is necessary to adjust the steering. They need to hold better discussions, so that experts can steer the country.

Now is also the perfect time for a world religion to develop

C
At first glance, Christianity and Islam seem to be in conflict, but we have actually been taught that, in the background, they are being guided by ninth dimensional beings that are branch spirits of El Cantare; Hermes guides Islam while Thoth guides Christianity, mainly in North America.

This might have to do with God's management, so please excuse me for sounding disrespectful, but is the conflict between Christianity and Islam occurring intentionally to have humanity realize something? Or, do Christianity and Islam each have things that they should repent for, and something that can overcome their opposition is being shown?

SHAKYAMUNI BUDDHA
This problem started after the transportation revolution and trade revolution that occurred in early modern history. It was important for each country to make progress. Right now, even a virus can affect the entire world as one unit, so it is only natural for the civilizations of the world to all be mixed together now. It is now time for the various aspects of these civilizations that developed in each region to make adjustments and show compromise. To put it another way, this is an age when even a virus can conquer the world, so it is also the perfect time for a world religion to develop.

B
Now is the perfect time for a world religion to develop?

SHAKYAMUNI BUDDHA
It wasn't possible in the past. Only local religions could develop. Shakyamuni Buddha was only able to preach as

far as he could walk. But that's not the case now. So, now is truly the time for a world religion to develop.

B
In that sense, then, the Golden Age is a time to overcome hardship and establish a new value standard...

SHAKYAMUNI BUDDHA
That's exactly right. And it is necessary to show that God is superior to AI, that God's wisdom surpasses AI. It is also a time when a world religion can be created. The virus has proven that.

8

People Are Being Tested to See Whether or Not They Have True Faith

The battle between light and darkness and the age of chaos will continue for some time

B

You just taught us that now is a time when a world religion can be created, but to me, it also seems like a period when light and dark are clashing. In other words, it is an opportunity to defeat darkness and establish a new world standard, but at the same time, it seems like darkness is getting stronger. But here is a major point of contention regarding that. As the infections continue to spread, humanity's fear has intensified, and a moment ago, you suggested that there may be witch hunts in which people displaying symptoms are instantly punished. When that happens, beings known as devils and evil spirits may take advantage of this and further develop a plan of darkness. Take the viral outbreak in Wuhan, China, as an example.

Right now, various spirits teach us that malicious space people are involved remotely, and behind the scenes, it appears that entities like them are hampering our efforts in undetectable ways. We would appreciate it if you could give us some hints, from the perspective of your devil-quelling, on what beings that control negative thoughts, like devils and evil spirits, are intending to do.

SHAKYAMUNI BUDDHA
The problem of malicious space people is the "next stage," so I will refrain from commenting on that. Humanity in general hasn't made it that far yet. It will still be quite a while before they reach the level where everyone believes in the existence of space people. Also, that is the "next stage," so I would first like to focus on the human level. I believe that this age of chaos between light and darkness will last for some time.

If it were possible to prevent these viral infections spreading in Japan using nothing more than a cloth mask, as Prime Minister Abe says, then there would be no need for religion. But in reality, viruses cannot be blocked by a cloth mask. There will soon be a limit to human wisdom.

They are telling people to "shelter in place" at home, but everyone will wither and die if they just stay at home and do nothing.

Also, in about another month, you will realize that the government won't be able to provide compensation for loss of earnings. That will become clear. Then, what should you do? I am sure that the battle between light and darkness as well as this age of chaos will continue for some time. However, they are also necessary in order to change today's politicians, the mass media, and public opinion.

If this were the kind of problem that could be overcome using the judgment they acquired through study and education, then this would just be considered a minor problem. What this means is that this will not be overcome through medicine, science, or education. The power of God will then take effect. At the same time, devils will also be active, but the power of God will begin to work. This age of chaos will continue for some time.

Even if this pathogen is stopped from spreading further and the number of people who get pneumonia and die drops, and even if you can get the situation under control to some extent, economically, there will follow a lengthy global recession. The chaos will continue. Not even Happy Science will make it through unscathed. With most believers staying at home, shops closing, and companies shutting down, not even Happy Science will come through this unharmed. Terrible things are sure to happen, and you have to fight through them.

How should we think about miracles?

A

I would like to ask a question about miracles. There are records of an incident that happened while you were alive. There was a plague running rampant in the town of Vaishali. It is said that, at that time, you purified the entire town, and quelled the disease. Modern priests and religious scholars, however, consider this to be a myth, but I believe that you were capable of performing those types of miracles. Of course, I understand that this virus has been given to humanity as a trial, but if you are aware of any method we could use to resist this virus, we would appreciate it if you could tell us.

SHAKYAMUNI BUDDHA

That's the kind of question that someone who still looks at things from the worldly perspective would ask. Everyone dies. Without a doubt, all people in Japan as well as in the world will die at some point. Very few people alive right now will live to see the 22nd century. Even if the virus doesn't kill them, they will die somehow. About a third of the people in Japan die from cancer. Together with heart and blood vessel-related illnesses, that accounts for half of all deaths. The virus will only account for a small portion of the causes of death. There is no fundamental solution because this world is not eternal. It is nothing more than a place for soul training.

Japan isn't as small as Vaishali, though. Japan is not really that small. To put it in terms of modern Japan, the power to purify Vaishali would be the equivalent of purifying Minato Ward, a district in the 23 special wards of Tokyo.

Japan is much larger than that, so I don't think it would be easy. Right now, though, ever since last year, many miracles have been occurring. I think there have been numerous miracles involving Happy Science. Miracles are miracles, I mean, unlike medicine, they don't work for everything. But at critical points, I am sure that miracles will occur for those who need them. In that sense, when it comes to your rightfulness and validity as a religion, I am sure you will be given a tailwind.

Happy Science has grown to expand the scope of its activities on a global scale, so your members won't be free of infections, and not every single member possesses deep faith. Some people will get infected, even within Happy Science.

However, among those, some will miraculously get better. Over the next several years, I am sure that you will witness the effects of the true Law of Cause and Effect that governs those things, which is different from the law of causality in this world. And in doing so, you will probably realize that faith and prayer possess actual power.

It is not possible to save everyone because everyone eventually dies. Death is unavoidable. And people don't really get to choose how they die. So, ultimately, there is nothing you can do about it. It's just a matter of how meaningfully you use the time given to you and how well you use it to improve your soul.

People are sometimes saved by miracles. But those cases must not conclude with mere materialistic joy. When miracles happen, I want you to realize that you are witnessing the glory of God, and that the recipients of such miracles are expected to achieve things worth those miracles. If you pray and are miraculously healed, you must not let that be the end of it. Those who are bestowed miracles need to reveal the glory of God to others. I would like for you to take this to heart.

The God of Genesis will never succumb to bat venom

B
This is related to the previous question. Recently, on April 11 (2020), Master Ryuho Okawa bestowed us with a prayer, "Prayer for New Resurrection." We are very thankful.

The prayer contains the following passages. "By dint of Your guidance, / We can believe we are also light in essence. / This alone is New Birth, / New Resurrection." and "Please allow me to wish for New Resurrection / Of my life and my body."

We were given a prayer to that effect, and the meaning is that some people are experiencing miracles, and this spreads the glory of God. We must achieve new resurrection for our souls while living in this materialistic society, and just now, you taught us that we need to realize our original self and learn who we truly are.

When striving to come to realizations to help us learn who we are and achieve new resurrection, Happy Science members illuminate ourselves based on teachings and the Truth. I believe that the general public and all of humanity will similarly wake up through learning such laws, but how can we come to realizations to help us become aware of our true selves? What sort of mindset should we hold to make it easiest for us to gain opportunities to awaken to the Truth?

SHAKYAMUNI BUDDHA
Developing faith requires more than just registering as a member. Faith is not proven just by paying for and experiencing prayers. There are different levels of faith. And I think that people are tested to see whether or not they have true faith. People are tested to see whether or not they

believe with all their heart that El Cantare is truly the God of the Earth, that El Cantare is truly the Primordial God, and that He has truly been guiding humanity from time immemorial. If El Cantare has been guiding humanity as the being responsible for having created humans on Earth, then there is no way He would succumb to something like a mere poisonous virus from a bat.

People who believe more in the power of bat toxin than in the power of El Cantare are weak, and Happy Science is not so weak that it has to protect even those who believe that bat venom is more powerful than El Cantare. It is necessary already to get over the desire to obtain worldly benefits from following teachings.

People have to realize that the God of Genesis possesses that much strength, and they should understand that He is something beyond the statue of Buddha enshrined in Horyuji Temple.

First, produce 10 times the number of true believers in Japan

A
Thank you very much for your valuable teachings today on a variety of issues. We intend to turn over a new leaf and face this crisis, devote ourselves to spiritual discipline, and further intensify our activities.

SHAKYAMUNI BUDDHA
First, it is important to produce 10 times the number of true believers in Japan.

A
Thank you very much for today.

B & C
Thank you very much.

RYUHO OKAWA
OK. [*Claps twice.*]
    The conversation covered a diverse range of topics, so I am sure it will serve as a useful reference.

CHAPTER TWO

Spiritual Messages from John Lennon

*Originally recorded in Japanese on April 14, 2020,
in the Special Lecture Hall of Happy Science in Japan,
and later translated into English.*

** This spiritual message was recorded in the morning of the day
"Shakyamuni Buddha's Future Prediction" (Chapter One) was recorded.*

John Lennon (1940 - 1980)

John Lennon was a British rock singer who was born in Liverpool. After several changes to their band name, the Beatles was formed in 1960. He played a central role in the band and composed many of their songs and lyrics. In 1964, "I Want to Hold Your Hand" became hugely successful in the United States, exploding into a Beatles boom occurring across the globe. After their disbanding in 1970, John Lennon went to the United States and worked solo there. While mainly working there on his music, he continued sending numerous messages to the world, including about the peace movement that he and his wife, Yoko Ono, both were involved in. He was shot dead in 1980.

1

The Spirit of John Lennon Talks about the World's Future

A smaller population will lead to fewer wars

(Editor's Note: the original recording of *Wanderer*, written and sung by Master Ryuho Okawa, spiritually supported by the spirit of John Lennon, is playing in the background.)

JOHN LENNON
This is John Lennon.

D
Oh, Mr. John Lennon is here.

JOHN LENNON
Yes. You can't repel anything using my song.

D
Do you mean the coronavirus?

JOHN LENNON

Yes. You can't. No way. I mean, the mission is to have people die. So, it can't be helped.

D

Oh, (die) of the virus, right?

JOHN LENNON

It is meant to reduce the population, so there's no use saying anything about it.

D

Is it better not to resist?

JOHN LENNON

Dying is the goal, right? China's population needs to be reduced, and if the population in other places are reduced as well, the world will become a little more peaceful. So, it can't be helped.

D

So, since the world is headed for war, people are being "removed." Is that right?

JOHN LENNON

If the virus runs rampant in developed countries and the populations there decrease, wars will occur less often. People will be sick of wars because they will see piles of corpses here and there. You can't stop this anymore.

D

I see.

JOHN LENNON

So, even if you ask me to make new ritual prayers and songs, they won't be effective. People will lose their jobs and go back to living primitively. That's also important.

The development of science will only cause wars. This time, people will realize how empty medical progress is. Too high of a population is the cause. Being a doctor has become the most dangerous occupation. Someday, no one will want to be a doctor.

D

That's true.

JOHN LENNON

Then, there will be no nurses. We will also... Those who hold concerts will all lose their jobs. We'll all go back to the primitive age. That will lead to a world of equality. We will all need to produce flour and grow vegetables for a living.

D

Now, human beings have become too materialistic.

JOHN LENNON

All animals are already infected too. You won't be able to eat meat anymore. You will have no choice but to be a yoga hermit. No one will listen to songs now. It's over.

The novel coronavirus and YouTube are similar

JOHN LENNON

I'm thinking of crushing YouTube as well.

D

I see. Some content is indeed terrible.

JOHN LENNON

It's already a virus too. It's spreading "viruses" too much.

D

That's true.

JOHN LENNON

Its users are spreading information without any official authorization. That's not good. It's a virus.

D

There are no rules.

JOHN LENNON

YouTube has mutated into the coronavirus, so they are the same.

D

But now, everyone is at home, surfing the internet.

JOHN LENNON

You should crush it all. You don't need it. You don't need it at all. Don't post your own personal tweets. You know?

D
You're right.

JOHN LENNON
Garbage.

D
Many meaningless things are posted and people are spending money advertising through them. This is really unbelievable.

JOHN LENNON
It's really a waste of time and a waste of life.

Songs shouldn't be streaming endlessly. You just need to listen to songs by proficient people. The rest is a waste of life for anyone. So, it's fine for karaoke shops to go bankrupt. You don't have to sing. It's meaningless for a poor singer to sing. All the useless work will disappear from now on. Right now, video-sharing websites are profitable, but soon, they will face a backlash. They will be in trouble. It'll become hard enough just to live. And, it is like a bubble. Ultimately, it's like a bubble; it's meaningless. Everyone is wasting their time doing meaningless things. It can't be helped.

Coronavirus: an alarm to awaken people to the truth that everything passes by?

D
You're right. People talk about democracy, but it's become a world where individuals are allowed to say anything they want. I feel something is wrong here.

JOHN LENNON
Human rights are important, but if they go too far, people will be like locusts. They will be hated. The coronavirus is meant to reduce the Earth's population to some level. So, it is like a "Buddhist prayer" to make people realize the impermanence of life.

OK? It is teaching that everything passes by. This world is transient. Do you know what I mean? You may have hope as you live in this world, but you will soon die saying good-bye.

D
That's true.

JOHN LENNON
Now is the time for Buddhism.

D

I see.

JOHN LENNON

"Impermanence of all things." "The egolessness of all phenomena."

D

How should we live then?

JOHN LENNON

Oh, you should just enter "the perfect tranquility of nirvana." Just be done with this world. You can go back to the other world saying, "I will never be reborn again."

D

I see.

JOHN LENNON

Your suffering increases all the more because you come back to this world. Enter nirvana at age 40… Oh, some people are past that age.

D

That's right. The lyrics of the song you assisted in writing* say, "She will disappear like a bubble."

JOHN LENNON

Of course. It's a bubble. Romantic love is like a bubble. It's ridiculous. Children aren't worth having. They all end up being good for nothing.

D

Umm...

JOHN LENNON

No. There's no need. You don't need children. You really don't need them. If the population is reduced to four billion, it would be refreshing.

D

Half of what it is now?

---

* Here, D is referring to the song, *Tokimeki-no-Toki* (literally, "Time of Love"). Words and music by Master Ryuho Okawa (assisting spirit: John Lennon). It is an insert song in a documentary film, *Living in the Age of Miracles* (planned by Master Ryuho Okawa), which was released late August 2020 in Japan.

JOHN LENNON
I'm not sure if Jesus has different thoughts, but the population increase poses a danger. It's dangerous, you know. Food problems, energy problems, war-related issues, and now infection problems. Over-population is the cause of all these problems. So, now you are told not to meet others, right?

Don't meet people. Then, there will need to be a lower population density, to the point that people won't see each other. So, the population will be reduced. It definitely will. It should.

Cholera ran rampant too. The Black Death and cholera. The Plague. The coronavirus is another one. It won't stop here. It cannot be helped. So, no one can go out. Everyone has nothing to do. They cannot make a living, so they will fall to poverty, and will all become beggars.

D
I see.

JOHN LENNON
People should go to big business companies and beg. Everyone should go to Bill Gates with a bowl for begging.

He should be able to care for many. He can disperse his over-accumulated money all around.

"There's no way you can protect yourself with a cloth mask"

JOHN LENNON
There's no way you can protect yourself with a cloth mask.

D
No.

JOHN LENNON
Viruses are even smaller. Face masks can keep out bacteria, but not viruses. So, it's ridiculous to wear masks. Masks won't block anything. Masks can keep saliva from being sprayed, that's all. So, viruses won't be blocked. Cloth masks have a low fiber density, so the virus comes in from everywhere.

D
I think Mr. R. A. Goal said the same thing.

JOHN LENNON

Yes, so, the only solution is to lower the population density. More people will die in developed countries because they have a higher population density. Manhattan, too. There are eight million people in such a small area (New York City). So, people will die. Silly.

2

The Idea That a Population Decline Would Bring World Peace

The coronavirus will spread on Chinese navy vessels and nullify military power

D
How about China?

JOHN LENNON
Umm?

D
What will happen to China? Will a swarm of locusts fly there?

JOHN LENNON
Something else will become prevalent in China. Anyway, we are planning to stop them from taking over foreign countries and doing bad things. So, I think we will

continue until we realize this goal. China's battered ships and aircraft carriers, will all be hit by the coronavirus. They have bad ventilation. The submarine crew members will catch it, too. Isn't it better that they're incapacitated by the virus? It will end without even having to fight. If carriers become like healthcare facilities where in-hospital infections occur, the submarine crew will all die out from the virus, assuming they stay submerged for a year.

D
Military weapons one after another...

JOHN LENNON
The trend is toward realizing peace through population decrease, so in my opinion, ritual prayers and songs won't work anymore. There are too many undesirable people. It's too bad. Still, people cannot eat infected meat. Even human flesh is inedible.

D
Right. Humans are inedible.

JOHN LENNON

Also, it's pitiful, but in Africa, the locusts are eating away all the food.

D

Do you know Niangniang*?

JOHN LENNON

Actually, I heard of her recently.

D

So, China will experience misfortunes other than the virus, right?

JOHN LENNON

[*Singing.*] "Power to the Niangniang ♪" Should I write a song like that?

D

[*Laughs.*]

---

* The Chinese goddess who was mentioned in the spiritual message, "Warning of the Next Crisis from Zulu, a Vengeful God in Africa," which was recorded on April 6, 2020. She is considered a horrifying Grim Reaper with a beautiful face.

JOHN LENNON
I'll use your face.

D
No thank you [*laughs*].

JOHN LENNON
Niangniang.

D
Niangniang.

JOHN LENNON
Pat pat.

In the eyes of the heavenly world, worthless things are popular in this world

D
So, you mean, we can't stop this trend?

JOHN LENNON
It's better for people to die. If the population of Japan drops to about 80 million, it will be a more peaceful country. That is almost the same as the population of Germany. When the population grows, Mr. Abe will act in a totalitarian way to seek for food and energy.

D
I see.

JOHN LENNON
That's for sure. So, it's better for the population not to increase.

People should just listen to the Beatles at home. Sorry, but the "extra" people will need to die. This is what Reapers and Archangels both are wishing for, so it can't be helped.

Even to us, we see 5,000, or 10,000, or even 70,000 people gathering and cheering for worthless music. It makes me want to spray insecticide over them. I want to say, "You idiots! Just die!" Don't make worthless music popular. That's my point. For example, there are groups like AKB, Nogizaka, or Keyakizaka in which members sing and dance together, so they will be affected by the coronavirus and will disband soon.

D
Too crowded, you mean?

JOHN LENNON
Yes. Then the world would become peaceful. Only good solo singers should sing.

D
It's true that there aren't many good singers, unlike in the past.

JOHN LENNON
This collectivism is coming to an end. I think it's good.

The Communist Party's one-party rule naturally brings confusion in a country where the population is increasing so much. Even democracy only works in a small country. If the population increases too much, it becomes quite difficult. People will be "egocratic." The more children you have, the more they become self-centered.

D
True, everyone becomes individualistic and says whatever they want, which ironically invites totalitarianism.

JOHN LENNON
There needs to be suppression. I'm sorry, but I have the same opinion as Niangniang.

D
But this is heaven's will.

JOHN LENNON
I want to knock them out.

D
I guess that, in the eyes of God or angels, this world has

become a place where people have degraded themselves so too much.

JOHN LENNON
Yes, their quality has dropped. The reason why people do not listen to the media but instead talk a lot on YouTube is that the media itself has no backbone anymore. They lack the backbone of justice. Without the standards to tell good from evil, every TV station just reports how many people died of the coronavirus. They're useless.

D
People appearing on TV are expressing different opinions, but they have no authority. The TV stations chose them arbitrarily.

JOHN LENNON
The Painted Skin*, right?

---

* *The Painted Skin* is a short story included in *Strange Tales from a Chinese Studio*, a collection of classical Chinese mysterious tales by Pu Songling during the Qing dynasty. The story depicts a specter who wears human skin and turns into a beautiful woman. Happy Science will release a film, *Utsukushiki-Yuwaku-Gendai-no-"Gahi"* (Literally, "Beautiful Temptation: The Modern 'Painted Skin'") (Executive producer and original story by Ryuho Okawa) in Japan, in 2021. The story is set in the present and reveals the true enlightenment of beauty using the subject of specters.

D

Maybe they are. There must be a lot of them.

JOHN LENNON

They're just pretty-faced, good-looking people.

D

The celebrities are on TV just for show, so we do not know their ideas or creeds. We do not know if they are really righteous in the eyes of God and Buddha.

Are viruses the shadow of the minds of humans, who have multiplied too much?

JOHN LENNON

You know, we're reflecting on this. Humankind looks like a swarm of locusts. Anyway, the population is about to quadruple compared to what it was about 100 years ago, and there surely is a limit to population growth. It cannot exceed 10 billion, no matter what. So, it will reach the limit, definitely.

Even if you could avoid the coronavirus, the next thing will come. I'm sure. We have prepared things in several stages. First, people living near the sea or at sea level will all be killed in disasters like rising sea levels or massive tsunamis. Next, if they escape up into the mountains thinking it is safe, volcanoes will erupt and those living there will all be killed. During harvest season, locusts will fly in swarms and eat everything. It will become like Pompeii with people becoming like Niangniang buried in hardened ashes. I'm sorry to say this, but God doesn't have the power to feed this population. So, He wishes that the population would decrease. It can't be helped. Look at the EU; about 30 countries have come together, but they all talk in different languages, so they can't understand each other. They must stop being different ethnic groups.

D
Right, they need to do things by themselves a little more…

JOHN LENNON
They're trying to make a "cooperative union," right?

D

Yes. They should stop relying on nations that have money.

JOHN LENNON

They are focusing on the disparity too much.

D

Yes.

JOHN LENNON

It's easier to make everyone poor than to make them wealthy. That is easy. It is hard to make everyone wealthy. If you try to make everyone wealthy, you will invite inflation. Money will be scattered and it will become worthless pieces of paper. So, it is easy to make everyone poor by making people unable to work, like how Mr. Abe and other leaders are doing now. They are telling people to stay at home. People in New York are told to stay at home all the time, which can only mean death. They will have no income and no food. It's the same as the Great Depression. So, there's nothing you can do.

Gods themselves have agreed to that, so the world is just going to become peaceful. Let's just reduce the population and make a peaceful world. And, people from advanced countries that "only consume in vast quantities" will be the first to die. Many will die.

For example, look at Africa. People there die, but it's hard to tell how many, no matter how many of them die. They don't even go to the hospital. They cannot walk tens of kilometers to the hospital. When someone dies, they just burn and bury them.

There would also be a disaster if war breaks out. Should a nuclear war occur, it would be terrible because the world would be contaminated with radiation. The hospitals will need to deal with a great number of patients with leukemia.

So, whatever people choose, they will die. There seem to be many stages prepared. People have reproduced a little too much. They are like viruses. Viruses are the shadow of the human mind.

3

Rock and Roll for Humankind, Who Have Little Faith

The higher the population, the higher the number of nonbelievers

D

It seems to me that materialism, atheism, and communist thinking have become so prevalent that people have covered the Earth like molds and viruses.

JOHN LENNON

They should just die. In the U.S., especially in New York, the number of leftists has grown. The West Coast has more leftists too. Many are going to die from the virus in these areas. If not, the West Coast will sink in the ocean or see a volcanic eruption. We must weed out some art, too. Hellish art will be weeded out. I'm sorry to say this, but you may be doing your last job now. Humankind will perish. Let's all enter Nirvana. It's your last job. Yes.

Bye-bye. Bye-bye, humanity. Bye-bye. Listen to my music and say bye-bye to the world.

D
You mean, you'll make a song titled, "Bye-bye"…

JOHN LENNON
[*Starts singing.*] Bye-bye ♪ Bye-bye ♪ Farewell, humanity ♪
Bye-bye ♪
Your age was really over in the 20th century ♪
But you lived well into the 21st century ♪
For this sin, you will be disinfected ♪
Bye-bye ♪

D
You mean, humanity has been making the wrong choices?

JOHN LENNON
The more the population grows, the more nonbelievers there are, right now.

D
That's right.

The world is getting tougher on people

JOHN LENNON
Islam, too, they no longer know who their God is. They distinguish themselves from others by calling themselves Muslims, but they don't know who God is. So, they are no good. So is China. They should be killed by Niangniang. OK?

In Christianity, too, they are highly educated in college and enjoying high incomes, but they all lack faith in God. They go to church only on Sundays, as a ritual, but it's mostly elderly people who go to church. Younger people will soon stop going.

You may face a situation in which you feel as if the Devil's Night has come. But you'll be better off after a while. You can recreate from scratch. You all have gone too far. Bye-bye.

D

You mean, we have been choosing the wrong thoughts to follow.

JOHN LENNON

The Beatles was allowed to fill stadiums with audiences. But many others are not allowed to do that. Ordinary people shouldn't do that. There are too many extra people. You know, you only need as many people to do the work required. More and more people drop out of school, bully others, and either work part-time or remain unemployed and live off their parents. This means the world is getting tougher on people. It's an age of salt and plums.

D

Wow...!

JOHN LENNON

What you need now are salt and plums. Now is the age when you must live on pickled plums. If you try to stay away from doing bad things, you had better climb up on a mountain and practice Zen meditation there. Something like that. It's because everything that people do is harmful. So, humans are no longer needed.

Looking from outer space far, far above, people running around on the ground and walking quickly through intersections all look like viruses. You should know that you're always seen that way and that we don't intend to feed the human race if it's just going to end up expanding hell.

Now, having more people means making larger hell. It's obvious. We need to be tougher. They have to learn only the good things. That's our idea.

What if John Lennon were to sing rock now?

JOHN LENNON
So, even if they listen to my songs, they won't recover from the viral infection.

D
I see.

JOHN LENNON
Because they must die. But of course, I can't say this out loud.

God is cunningly preparing such Grim Reapers. He makes it look like it is the work of Grim Reapers, not His work. It can't be helped, I guess. Talking about your five children, one of them has dropped out. That's the way things are. They must be removed.

D
I guess what Hiroshi did* became the decisive factor in causing the coronavirus outbreak.

JOHN LENNON
You can say it's the "Hiroshi virus." In the time when the God of humankind lives on Earth, if someone appears and pours feces from a cesspool on Him, the virus will put an end to all of them.

---
* Since 2018, Hiroshi Okawa, the author's eldest son, has been receiving strong but negative spiritual influence. He has repeatedly defamed Happy Science based on false claims and delusions, on his YouTube videos and a book published by Bungeishunju. Thus, Happy Science filed a lawsuit against him for defamation.

D

Hiroshi is a lost cause. He must not express his delusions as if they were fact.

JOHN LENNON

A lot of the mass media will close up shop, too. Unfortunately, anything that has enjoyed prosperity and become arrogant will close.

That's fine. I think you need to make something good from scratch. For a long time in the history of humankind, there have only been hundreds of millions of people. For a really long time. Now, there's a bubble boom, so the quality of the souls has degraded. All they do is demand their rights.

D

I see. That's right.

JOHN LENNON

Humanity was done after the age of the Beatles. It will be more troublesome if there are more people, so we have created a situation where people can't gather anymore.

D

I understand.

JOHN LENNON

So, if I were to sing a rock song now, it would be like, "Let's die of the coronavirus." "Let's hit the road and die!" "Go out into crowds every day and you all are going to die ♪"

D

It is surely "rock" in this situation.

JOHN LENNON

It will be a song like, "If you want your pension, walk around looking for a crowd ♪" [*Laughs.*]

It's OK. A life of 50 years is long enough. They live too long. It's enough. Even their children won't support them. Children won't look after their parents, so governments must support them, but they won't last. It can't be helped. The elderly may die first. It's OK, just let it go.

Many people are dying in hospitals. Doctors who graduated from difficult medical schools earn higher incomes and have become arrogant. Such "deviation value-oriented" prosperity will end. They don't deserve that much respect in the first place.

It's OK because diseases exist to shorten life spans. To fight diseases is to oppose God. So, if you get sick, you had better die gracefully. "So, you are all♪ stupid boys and girls♪ bye-bye♪"

D
You mean, for God, human beings are all bad children...

JOHN LENNON
Yes.

D
I see.

What will happen to the leaders of the U.S., U.K., and Germany?

JOHN LENNON
So, people have almost lost their faith in God.

D

I see. It's true.

JOHN LENNON

All they want are food, fuel, power, and reputation. That's not good.

D

They are spitting in their parent's (God's) face.

JOHN LENNON

And, a prosperous country of white people, in reflection for their years of exploitation based on slavery, will end up like the Egyptians who were killed by Yahweh.

D

Oh, that's what it means.

JOHN LENNON

Yes.

D

On hearing it, I kind of felt sorry for them, even though Mr. Trump is their president.

JOHN LENNON

Mr. Trump may be infected, eventually.

D

Really?

JOHN LENNON

Yes. It can't be helped. The end will come. Give it back to the Native Americans. So...

D

I am wondering if there is any meaning behind British Mr. Johnson's miraculous resurrection.

JOHN LENNON

He is still young.

D

I see.

JOHN LENNON

He is still young. His spirit happened to come over here and enter the body of Master Ryuho Okawa.* Then, he was recharged with light.

D

He definitely received light. Indeed.

JOHN LENNON

Yes, maybe. That's why he was able to leave the hospital.

D

The timing really makes me think so.

JOHN LENNON

It's his resurrection. He had faith in God.

D

It's absolutely because his soul entered the body of Master Okawa.

---

* See Appendix: "Search for Real Intensions of Prime Minister Boris Johnson and Chancellor Angela Merkel" in *Jesus Christ's Answers to the Coronavirus Pandemic* (Tokyo: HS Press, 2020).

JOHN LENNON
He has faith.

D
If I say this, everyone will try to enter Master.

JOHN LENNON
Oh, that's no good. Merkel came to get recharged, too.

D
She did.

JOHN LENNON
Yes. Merkel is now gaining popularity. You know? Hahahahahaha. [*Laughs.*]

A world in which John Lennon was shot dead must not continue to prosper

JOHN LENNON
We sometimes need to change the values of the world. Time passes, and people should know that they can do nothing about it.

D

Right, you were born in the ruins of World War II.

JOHN LENNON

That's right.

D

It must have been a pretty miserable world at that time.

JOHN LENNON

I was only allowed to live for about 40 years. A world in which John Lennon was shot dead must not continue to prosper.

D

No, it must not.

JOHN LENNON

Right. So, there will be some kind of reaction at work.

D

I understand.

JOHN LENNON

John Lennon was shot dead and Mandela was confined in prison for 27 years. Gandhi was assassinated, too. People are no good, really.

D

I agree. Many ninth dimensional grand spirits were punished by humanity.

JOHN LENNON

Humans are idiots beyond control. They all are out of control.

D

It's a bad human race.

JOHN LENNON

Yes. So, it's over. You too, Que Sera Kera. It's Que Sera Kera.

D

Que Será Será*?

---

* A Spanish phrase that means, "Whatever will be, will be." *Que Será Será* was well known in the 1950s as the theme song of an American film, *The Man Who Knew Too Much* (Paramount Pictures, 1956).

JOHN LENNON
It's Que Será Será. Yes, that's right. We are not free in this world, but we are free in the other world. Let's go back to the other world!

D
That's a Buddhist thought.

JOHN LENNON
Yes. Buddhism. Now is the time to have Buddha extinguish you all. "Prayer to Extinguish Humankind."

D
Oh.

JOHN LENNON
Hmph. Truly.

4

Heaven's Will in the Eyes of the Spirit of John Lennon

"The population won't grow so much anymore"

JOHN LENNON

Foxes are already gone. That's why they come out and bite your butt as spirits.

(Interviewer's Note: Master Ryuho Okawa conducted a spiritual reading on the cause of the pain that had lasted for several days on the left side butt of the interviewer, and found that foxes dispatched by the nine-tailed fox had possessed her in turns. It seemed they came to fight against the production of a Happy Science film, *Utsukushiki-Yuwaku-Gendai-no-"Gahi"* (Literally, "Beautiful Temptation: The Modern 'Painted Skin'") and tried to disturb the film shooting. Since it is a rare spiritual phenomenon, we decided to publish it as it is.)

Actually, they want to be born as human beings.

D
I see.

JOHN LENNON
They want to enter the human body. If the number of human beings increases, they will come in. But I won't allow them to do so.

D
You mean, the spirits of foxes biting my butt in turns?

JOHN LENNON
Yes, that's right. They all want to be reborn as human beings.

D
Oh, is that it?

JOHN LENNON
They want to be born as human females and seduce people.

D

But since they have to store up their spiritual power, it's hard for them to be reborn as human beings. Is that right?

JOHN LENNON

Yes. So, the population won't grow so much anymore.

D

I see.

JOHN LENNON

We don't need them. We don't. No.

"In the end, space people will begin to attack from outer space"

JOHN LENNON

In the end, or next, space people will begin to attack from outer space. I want to give you a break, but when a space war begins, there's no way you can win because your scientific technology is behind theirs by more than 1,000 years.

D
Earth's technology can't match up to theirs.

JOHN LENNON
No. In the past, someone wrote a story about aliens dying of a virus. But what is happening now is that a virus is killing people on Earth. Things have turned out to be the opposite.

D
In the film starring Tom Cruise[*], aliens died of the virus on Earth.

JOHN LENNON
But when a virus spreads and humans die, the Reptilians won't be able to eat humans.

D
I see. It's well-thought-out.

JOHN LENNON
Yes.

---
[*] *War of the Worlds* (Paramount Pictures, 2005). It is based on a classic science fiction novel by H.G. Wells.

D

I see. It's true.

The civilization based on reason and intelligence is about to bring an end to humanity

JOHN LENNON

I guess that you see the year 2020 as...

D

The Golden Age.

JOHN LENNON

The Golden Age. The Golden Age means, "the period of mowing greens." Hahaha. [*Laughs.*]

D

I guess it can't be helped, since no matter how hard Master Okawa worked, humankind didn't listen to him.

JOHN LENNON

Not even 100 million people would listen anyway, right? They're no good at all.

D

They all see themselves as gods.

JOHN LENNON

They forgot God, so you can't do anything about it. Godless children just do a part-time job and starve to death. It can't be helped. We don't need children who don't listen to their parents. We don't need children who don't listen to God.

D

They can't even thank their parents (God).

Shakyamuni Buddha talked about miracles in his spiritual messages.* He said that in essence, the human race won't be able to live on Earth without an unbelievably well-balanced environment. He talked about something like that.

---

* Refer to Ryuho Okawa, *Buddha-wa-Kiseki-o-dou-Kangaeru-ka* (literally, "What Does Buddha Think of Miracles?") (Tokyo: IRH Press, 2020).

JOHN LENNON

The "super-spoiled democracy" is over. You must live on only "salt" and "plums." You need to live on salt, plum, and kelp only. It has been said that human history will end with democracy. Now, the end has come.

Unless people live their lives as children of God, the world will end. You have already sent out enough messages. Although the virus has spread, God's teachings won't spread?

D

No.

JOHN LENNON

It can't be helped. This is what God does. The world will start all over again. It can't be helped. The sense of values will be turned upside down. That started with Immanuel Kant. After Kant, people created a reason-oriented civilization, and now the civilization created based on reason and intelligence is about to bring an end to humanity.

Just enjoy living in the primitive age. That will be better for you. Yes.

D

I understand.

Bad people need to reflect on themselves

JOHN LENNON

I'm sorry. There's no way to save you anymore.

D

It really is heaven's will, I guess?

JOHN LENNON

Yes, it is.

D

I understand.

JOHN LENNON

You have no choice but to ask bad people to die first. So, at the onset, luxury cruise ships were full of rich, older people who contracted the virus. The pandemic must have spread from there. Next, crew members of aircraft carriers and submarines will get infected, too. The infection will spread further and further. Things made of a lot of money will perish. Sorry. I have to teach Niangniang how to cross the sea.

D
China still dispatches their warships to the waters off the coast of Taiwan, and they sank Vietnamese ships and are taking other provocative actions.

JOHN LENNON
They should suffer from food shortages. If that happens, they will have no time to do such things.

D
I see.

JOHN LENNON
Hmm. I think Taiwan and Hong Kong will be protected. Probably.

D
Ironically, you mean?

JOHN LENNON
They don't want to become like that. China is now hiding the truth. The truth is that they are in an even worse situation, I think.

D
Within China?

JOHN LENNON
Yes, yes.

D
I see.

JOHN LENNON
So, Japanese companies that have helped China a lot with its economic growth will go bankrupt from now. It can't be helped, since they did a bad thing. They have invited

national crises for the sake of their own profits. Nothing can be done about that.

And then, countries that have enslaved a large number of people need to reflect on themselves. They will become a bit weaker because they had everything their own way through enslaving others and destroying other countries. It can't be helped.

So, they need to shrink to the point that they no longer harm each other. This is an option. It will just look like each person inhales the virus and dies of pneumonia. It's not murder or anything else. They will die because they will get what they deserve. There is no way to prevent it. Cloth masks will be sent, but they are useless. The virus will pass through them. They are going back to being primitive people. Old politicians had better die early. They will start dying. They served their purpose.

The trigger and purpose of this turmoil

JOHN LENNON
The trigger for this trouble was your eldest son.

D

I thought so. He was terrible. He has gone too far against God.

JOHN LENNON

Your eldest son was a trigger.

D

That's unforgivable.

JOHN LENNON

Such atheistic hedonism, we won't forgive. That's why we have made hedonistic shops close now.

D

Weekly magazines are also taking advantage of what he's said.

JOHN LENNON

Right. We will destroy weekly magazines, too. So, we need to be tougher. It is important to make the best use of the selected few. That's what we mean. I am sorry for being "rock."

D

No, don't be.

JOHN LENNON

But these are my true thoughts.

D

Yes. I never expected that we would be able to speak to John Lennon.

JOHN LENNON

God doesn't like humans who kill ninth dimensional grand spirits, one after another, because they don't follow His words. That's what it's all about. And we don't want hell to expand any further.

D

If the situation stays as it is, hell will expand further and further. Far more than half of the people are likely to go to hell.

JOHN LENNON
Hmm. Most people will go to hell, I think. Because people are giving and receiving wrong educations now.

D
Yes.

JOHN LENNON
So, it is necessary to make them feel the limits of science and themselves. Space people have a type of science in which they believe in everything from God through to spiritual powers. That is what a more advanced science is like.

We are going to make the entire human race repent. This is our purpose. They all must repent to the point that they have no other choice but to pray to God in the face of severe calamity. Masks provide no defense. Until people pray to God, this will never end.

There is Niangniang in China, so you (D) must be like her in Japan. You will run amok in Japan. Wow!

It is enough for only the selected children to be born from now on. We don't need "extra people" to be born. OK?

D
I understand.

JOHN LENNON
Japan's suitable population is 80 million. Hahaha. [*Laughs.*]

D & E
Thank you very much.

RYUHO OKAWA
OK. [*Claps once.*]

It is said from ancient times that those who have attained enlightenment like Shakyamuni Buddha can use abilities beyond human knowledge freely at their will, namely the Six Divine Supernatural Powers (astral travel, clairvoyance, clairaudience, mind-reading, fate-reading, and spiritual wisdom). These spiritual abilities of the highest level transcend the boundaries of time and space, and enable one to freely see through the past, present, and future lives. Okawa is able to use these Six Divine Supernatural Powers freely and conduct various readings.

In the spiritual reading sessions compiled in this book, Okawa uses these abilities to conduct spiritual messages, spiritual vision, time-travel reading (seeing through the subject's past and future), remote-viewing (sending part of the spirit body to a specific location and seeing the situation there), mind-reading (reading the subject's thoughts and will, including those in a remote location), and mutual conversation (communicating with the thoughts of various beings that are beyond human contact).

CHAPTER THREE

Messages from Metatron and Yaidron

- UFO Reading 50 -

*Originally recorded in Japanese on April 14, 2020,
in the Special Lecture Hall of Happy Science in Japan,
and later translated into English.*

* *This UFO reading was recorded on the night of the day "Shakyamuni
Buddha's Future Prediction" (Chapter One) was recorded.*

Metatron

A space being from Planet Include in Sagittarius. A part of Jesus Christ's space soul (Amor). Born in Mesopotamia about 6,500 years ago. One of the gods of Light.

Yaidron

A space being from Planet Elder in the Magellanic Clouds. He is a powerful being with higher-dimensional powers in the Earth Spirit World and is a god of justice-like being. Yaidron is currently protecting Master Ryuho Okawa, the human incarnation of El Cantare, God of the Earth. He has been involved with the rise and fall of civilizations, wars, and major disasters on Earth.

1
Message from Metatron

"We are also one of the variables"
"I'm going to put an artistic end to this"

D

Please wait for a moment.

RYUHO OKAWA

It looks like it's in the west.

D

I found it.

RYUHO OKAWA

To the west?

D

Yes.

RYUHO OKAWA
I think it's Metatron. Metatron has appeared.

Is there anything you would like to say? Today, we recorded "Spiritual Messages from John Lennon" (Chapter Two) in the morning and "Shakyamuni Buddha's Future Prediction" (Chapter One) in the afternoon. May I ask why you are here today?

[*About five seconds of silence.*]

* *All texts in bold and quotation marks are the words of the space beings that Ryuho Okawa conducted readings on.*

RYUHO OKAWA
"**Last year was really tough, but this year is also really tough.**"

D
Yes.

RYUHO OKAWA
"**People on Earth have not yet realized that the variables Shakyamuni Buddha mentioned today include us. We**

are one of the variables. We are also considering where to stop the damage. As I said earlier this year*, eventually, I am going to put an artistic end to this. So, regarding that matter, please trust me.

"This year, everything will be rather slow and inactive, but we will make efforts to strengthen people's faith in God and start the age of new construction, new management, and new politics. So, from now on, you will see unexpected events in the world of politics, economy, and diplomacy. On each occasion, we will send you our messages, so you don't have to worry."

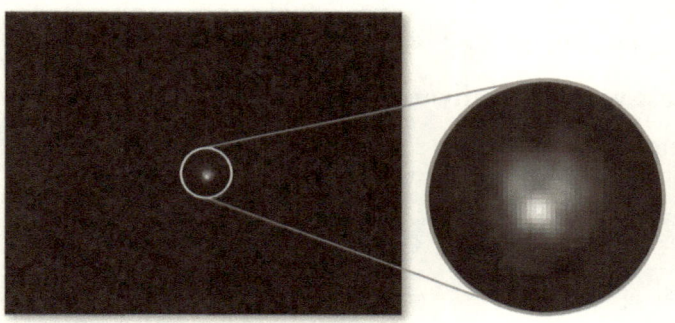

Metatron's UFO captured in this recording session
Spotted by Ryuho Okawa
April 14, 2020, at 10:21 pm in Tokyo
(Right: enlarged image)

Happy Science must be the last stronghold

RYUHO OKAWA
"You may have some worries about Happy Science itself, but don't worry. Happy Science will spread too like the virus. We are going to expand Happy Science to 10 times the size it is now."

D
We, Earthlings, need to work hard, right?

RYUHO OKAWA
"That is right. You have to give it your all. The disciples in particular must work hard. You might be underestimating the situation because you are able to live somewhat normally, but you are not always in peacetime.

"If you don't expand to 10 times the size you are now, you will not be able to fulfill your mission. You need to be 10 times as strong in Japan, as well. Happy Science must be strong in times of crisis. There will be political

---

* On January 2, 2020, Metatron came to give the New Year's greetings and send a message to the author. See *Spiritual Reading of Novel Coronavirus Infection Originated in China* (Tokyo: HS Press, 2020).

confusion, but you need to be tenacious. You must be the last stronghold. The final judgment for people to rely on—that is the work that the Master of Happy Science must do.

"This Age will definitely head in that direction. Please rely on us. We are also one of the variables, but a variable that doesn't need to be known. You, Happy Science, should express our opinions as your own to change the world. You are in a position to save the world.

"I won't allow the current Japanese politics to continue as it is, so more damage will be expected to some extent. When Japan reaches the stage where it begins to change, we will shift the overall direction.

"We can guarantee you that China will never stay as it is. I want to say this, at least."

D
Thank you very much.

RYUHO OKAWA
OK, then, let's ask Yaidron.

D

Yes.

RYUHO OKAWA

Over there, right?

D

Yes. Please hold on a second. OK, we would like to end the session with Metatron here.

RYUHO OKAWA

OK.

2
Message from Yaidron

Fear not the coronavirus

D
It's in frame.

RYUHO OKAWA
You got it? OK. Is it Yaidron? It is. He has appeared in the sky above us. This is the spot where we can see him most clearly.

D
Today, the two main figures have...

RYUHO OKAWA
Have appeared.

D
They are shining in the night sky.

RYUHO OKAWA

Yaidron, could you give us your message?

[*About five seconds of silence.*] "I am thinking, 'Fear not the coronavirus.' Today, Shakyamuni Buddha has told you, 'Can't you tell which is stronger, the power of the Original God, who is the God of Creation, or a bat-borne virulent virus?' This is an important message. People cannot be saved unless their faith reaches that level. The world cannot be saved.

"Just working as a founder of a religion or working in the category of religion is not enough.

"Recently, people say that the coronavirus situation will overwhelm the medical system. However, there are

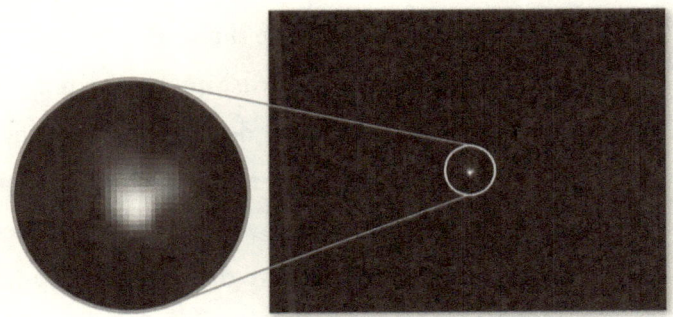

Yaidron's UFO captured in this recording session
Spotted by Ryuho Okawa
April 14, 2020, at 10:31 pm in Tokyo
(Left: enlarged image)

things that they have taken away from God. Hospitals surely have their own jobs, but they should give back what they took from God. We believe so.

"There are things beyond their power. That world is by far bigger. Regarding that world, religious leaders must lead people with their words. Doctors cannot judge anything and they are afraid to accept patients."

D
That's true.

RYUHO OKAWA
"They are afraid of getting infected just by accepting patients, so it's time for religious leaders to lead people. Religious leaders are born to save the world.

"From now on, various hardships and difficulties will occur worldwide, such as deaths due to illness, social turmoil, war, and great economic depression, but I believe Happy Science has the power to solve all of them.

"So, from now on, please have the capacity to admit 10, 20, or 100 times more believers. You are the last lighthouse that illuminates the world. It's important to let people know there is an existence who will never abandon the Earth."

People in Western countries and the Middle East will seek for the Real God

D
We, the believers and staff of Happy Science, need to do a deeper check of our faith.

RYUHO OKAWA
"Yes."

D
We hear more and more information based on worldly values, every day.

RYUHO OKAWA
"Yes, they have a big influence."

D

It means we need to think deeply about the Real Original God.

RYUHO OKAWA

"Yes. Western countries suffering from this coronavirus disaster are unstable, and they will continue to be so, but people will start to pray to the Real God. Furthermore, people in the Middle East, mainly from Iran, will seek for the Real God. I think the teachings of the Real God will spread."

D

So, you mean, it is important to think about the God who lies at the root of Jesus Christ?

RYUHO OKAWA

"Yes. People must know that when they pray to Jesus, their prayer reaches El Cantare. If that God didn't appear now, when else would He appear?

"Western people who believe in God know that He will appear in times of such global crises. Soon, they will realize His presence in Japan. Moreover, it will be proven that the power of faith can defeat illness.

"This year, there will occur various troubles, but you can definitely overcome them. We have come out and have been guarding you. We have never shown ourselves this much before. We are expressing our opinions clearly. We are the ultimate weapon. We will protect the Earth. We will, all the way through."

D
Thank you so much.

There exists the Original God of not only the Earth, but the universe

D
There are ethnic gods all over the world.

RYUHO OKAWA
"Yes, yes."

D

I think it's time for them to pray to the Original God, the World God.

RYUHO OKAWA

"Of course. Since long ago, people have believed that God exists in heaven, so they have mixed us, who are up in the sky, up with gods. But we are saying that we, who come from more advanced civilizations than Earth's and are protecting the Earth from up above, were also created by the God of the Earth long ago. This is the first time for such a thing to be revealed. It is the first time. This fact was revealed for the first time. It's incredible."

D

You mean, it's never been revealed so clearly before, so there are no books or records that can refer to it.

RYUHO OKAWA

"It's incredible. It surely is. There exists the Original God, who conveys the Laws of the Universe, which will probably be made into a Happy Science movie. He also governs us beings from outer space, who are mistaken for gods. Furthermore, not only is He the Original God of the Earth, but also of the universe. No one but us can prove this fact.

"So, from now on, we will enter the age when our presence will exert a certain influence on Earth. El Cantare's disciples cannot protect Him any longer, so we are protecting Him. We have entered such times.

"We have already stepped into the age of miracles. If people's faith gets stronger, more miracles will occur. Miracles that people have never seen, not just at a level of curing illness, but miracles of a greater scale.

"We expect you to have indomitable faith that is strong enough to bear the weight of such miracles. Even beings like us who have advanced scientific technology believe in God, so you should not be that weak."

D
I truly agree.

We are also fighting to prevent the future of the Earth from becoming confused

D

Allow me to move the camera a little. You mean, thinking of that God leads us to wonder why humans exist in the first place?

RYUHO OKAWA

"Yes. And people on Earth seem to be engaged only in battles with the misfortune happening on Earth, but in our world, we are already fighting a space war. We are currently fighting against evil aliens who are planning to invade the Earth. Since only Happy Science knows about this, I want to convey this.

"I want people to notice that we are on your team, fighting against evil aliens who plan to invade the Earth and bring confusion to its future."

D

Thank you so much.

RYUHO OKAWA

"In a sense, that is also the power of *Ame-no-Mioya-Gami**. I hope the day will come when the teachings spread more and more and Happy Science becomes stable enough so that Master Okawa can reveal the secrets of the universe.

"We possess plenty of future science. But we cannot just give it out. If people lose their faith or forget about God and spirits, the future science will instead be a waste and eventually destroy humankind. We will fight."

D

In the end, if you don't understand God, it's hard to tell right from wrong as a human.

RYUHO OKAWA

"Yes. Right."

---

* *Ame-no-Mioya-Gami* is the creator God who appears in an ancient Japanese text called *Hotsuma Tsutae*. According to Happy Science, he is the manifestation of El Cantare, the God of the Earth, in Japanese Shinto. He is also said to be the same spiritual being as the one who guided Jesus and whom Jesus called "Father". See *Ame-no-Mioya-Gami-no-Korin* (Literally, "Ame-no-Mioya-Gami's Descent") (Tokyo: IRH Press, 2019) and *The Laws of Faith* (New York: IRH Press, 2018).

D

You could have highly advanced scientific technology, but if you only ever use it for the wrong purposes, it would be better not to have it.

RYUHO OKAWA

"We want people to know the fact that we, who were mistaken for gods in heaven in ancient times, can communicate with El Cantare, who is living on earth right now. We want you to leave a record of this for your future generations.

"We will keep working hard, so please wait and see."

D

We, also, must make more efforts.

RYUHO OKAWA

"Yes. There will be things that you, disciples cannot do, but there are things that Metatron and Yaidron can. And, there are many others like R. A. Goal*, who have hidden power. Sooner or later, they will all join us too. They should be waiting for the time to come."

D

Thank you so much for helping us.

RYUHO OKAWA

"Yes, we can definitely win. Let's do our best."

D

Yes, thank you so much.

---

* A space being from Planet Andalucia Beta in Ursa Minor. One of the commanders of the space defense force. A certified messiah.

3

"Spiritual Messages from Shakyamuni Buddha" Revealed a Part of the True Thoughts of El Cantare

RYUHO OKAWA

Oh?

D

Something has appeared between them. It's between Yaidron and Metatron.

RYUHO OKAWA

Is it gone?

D

No, it's still there.

RYUHO OKAWA

It's still there. Is there anything else to say? Anything else?

[*About five seconds of silence.*] **"There are others, but think of them as your teammates."**

D
I see.

RYUHO OKAWA
They say, **"It's OK for today."**

D
OK, then, this concludes today's UFO reading on Metatron and Yaidron. Thank you so much. They came to give us encouragement.

RYUHO OKAWA
Was today's spiritual message (Chapter One) heavy?

D
Yes, it was.

RYUHO OKAWA
Some of the true thoughts of El Cantare were revealed.

D

Today's spiritual message was amazing. A part of the true thoughts of El Cantare was revealed. Thank you. This is the age of miracles.

RYUHO OKAWA

It is amazing that we have conversations with space people.

D

Truly it is, it's a miracle. I highly respect the level of faith that the space people have.

Afterword

Is the fear of infection and death caused by the coronavirus pandemic a blessing from God or a declaration of victory from the Grim Reaper? The answer will depend on how humanity takes it.

During his spiritual message, John Lennon appeared defiant on the surface, but if you carefully read and appreciate his true meaning, you will see an aspect of God's true intentions. To the Earth, this mass proliferation of humans in their rebellious age is like a global outbreak of a malignant virus.

To prevent yourself from becoming "darnel weed" that gets mowed down, you must become a person of love who is full of faith.

Illness is a trial that humanity cannot avoid. However, once illness has been overcome, on the other side, there exists the world of eternal life.

Entrust your life, not to a cloth mask, but faith in God.

>
> *Ryuho Okawa*
> *Master & CEO of Happy Science Group*
> *April 23, 2020*

ABOUT THE AUTHOR

RYUHO OKAWA was born on July 7th 1956, in Tokushima, Japan. After graduating from the University of Tokyo with a law degree, he joined a Tokyo-based trading house. While working at its New York headquarters, he studied international finance at the Graduate Center of the City University of New York. In 1981, he attained Great Enlightenment and became aware that he is El Cantare with a mission to bring salvation to all of humankind. In 1986, he established Happy Science. It now has members in over 110 countries across the world, with more than 700 local branches and temples as well as 10,000 missionary houses around the world. The total number of lectures has exceeded 3,200 (of which more than 150 are in English) and over 2,700 books (of which more than 550 are Spiritual Interview Series) have been published, many of which are translated into 31 languages. Many of the books, including *The Laws of the Sun* have become best sellers or million sellers. To date, Happy Science has produced 20 movies. The original story and original concept were given by the Executive Producer Ryuho Okawa. Recent movie titles are *The Real Exorcist* (live-action, May 2020), *Living in the Age of Miracles* (documentary, Aug. 2020), and *Twiceborn* (live-action, scheduled to be released in Oct. 2020). He has also composed the lyrics and music of over 150 songs, such as theme songs and featured songs of movies. Moreover, he is the Founder of Happy Science University and Happy Science Academy (Junior and Senior High School), Founder and President of the Happiness Realization Party, Founder and Honorary Headmaster of Happy Science Institute of Government and Management, Founder of IRH Press Co., Ltd., and the Chairperson of New Star Production Co., Ltd. and ARI Production Co., Ltd.

WHAT IS EL CANTARE?

El Cantare means "the Light of the Earth," and is the Supreme God of the Earth who has been guiding humankind since the beginning of Genesis. He is whom Jesus called Father and Muhammad called Allah. Different parts of El Cantare's core consciousness have descended to Earth in the past, once as Alpha and another as Elohim. His branch spirits, such as Shakyamuni Buddha and Hermes, have descended to Earth many times and helped to flourish many civilizations. To unite various religions and to integrate various fields of study in order to build a new civilization on Earth, a part of the core consciousness has descended to Earth as Master Ryuho Okawa.

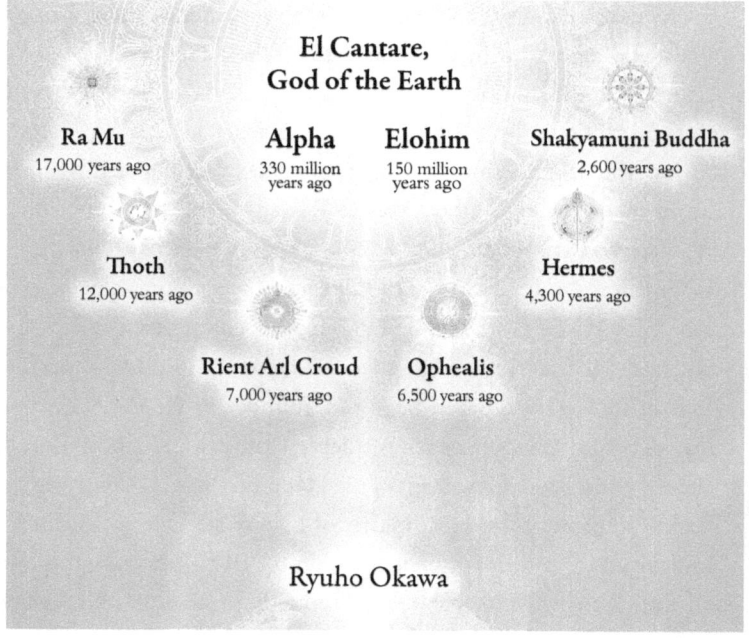

Alpha is a part of the core consciousness of El Cantare who descended to Earth around 330 million years ago. Alpha preached Earth's Truths to harmonize and unify Earth-born humans and space people who came from other planets.

Elohim is a part of El Cantare's core consciousness who descended to Earth around 150 million years ago. He gave wisdom, mainly on the differences of light and darkness, good and evil.

Shakyamuni Buddha was born as a prince into the Shakya Clan in India around 2,600 years ago. When he was 29 years old, he renounced the world and sought enlightenment. He later attained Great Enlightenment and founded Buddhism.

Hermes is one of the 12 Olympian gods in Greek mythology, but the spiritual Truth is that he taught the teachings of love and progress around 4,300 years ago that became the origin of the current Western civilization. He is a hero that truly existed.

Ophealis was born in Greece around 6,500 years ago and was the leader who took an expedition to as far as Egypt. He is the God of miracles, prosperity, and arts, and is known as Osiris in the Egyptian mythology.

Rient Arl Croud was born as a king of the ancient Incan Empire around 7,000 years ago and taught about the mysteries of the mind. In the heavenly world, he is responsible for the interactions that take place between various planets.

Thoth was an almighty leader who built the golden age of the Atlantic civilization around 12,000 years ago. In the Egyptian mythology, he is known as god Thoth.

Ra Mu was a leader who built the golden age of the civilization of Mu around 17,000 years ago. As a religious leader and a politician, he ruled by uniting religion and politics.

WHAT IS A SPIRITUAL MESSAGE?

We are all spiritual beings living on this earth. The following is the mechanism behind Master Ryuho Okawa's spiritual messages.

1 You are a spirit

People are born into this world to gain wisdom through various experiences and return to the other world when their lives end. We are all spirits and repeat this cycle in order to refine our souls.

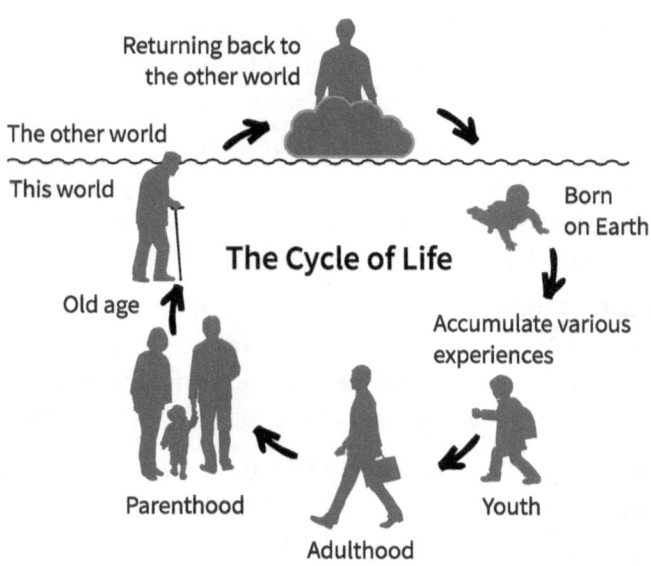

2 You have a guardian spirit

Guardian spirits are those who protect the people who are living on this earth. Each of us has a guardian spirit that watches over us and guides us from the other world. They were us in our past life, and are identical in how we think.

3 How spiritual messages work

Master Ryuho Okawa, through his enlightenment, is capable of summoning any spirit from anywhere in the world, including the spirit world.

Master Okawa's way of receiving spiritual messages is fundamentally different from that of other psychic mediums who undergo trances and are thereby completely taken over by the spirits they are channeling.

Master Okawa's attainment of a high level of enlightenment enables him to retain full control of his consciousness and body throughout the duration of the spiritual message. To allow the spirits to express their own thoughts and personalities freely, however, Master Okawa usually softens the dominancy of his consciousness. This way, he is able to keep his own philosophies out of the way and ensure that the spiritual messages are pure expressions of the spirits he is channeling.

Since guardian spirits think at the same subconscious level as the person living on earth, Master Okawa can summon the spirit and find out what the person on earth is actually thinking. If the person has already returned to the other world, the spirit can give messages to the people living on earth through Master Okawa.

Since 2009, more than 1,100 sessions of spiritual messages have been openly recorded by Master Okawa, and the majority of these have been published. Spiritual messages from the guardian spirits of people living today such as Donald Trump, Japanese Prime Minister Shinzo Abe and Chinese President Xi Jinping, as well as spiritual messages sent from the spirit world by Jesus Christ, Muhammad, Thomas Edison, Mother Teresa, Steve Jobs and Nelson Mandela are just a tiny pack of spiritual messages that were published so far.

Domestically, in Japan, these spiritual messages are being read by a wide range of politicians and mass media, and the high-level contents of these books are delivering an impact even more on politics, news and public opinion. In recent years, there have been spiritual messages recorded in English, and English translations are being done on the spiritual messages given in Japanese. These have been published overseas, one after another, and have started to shake the world.

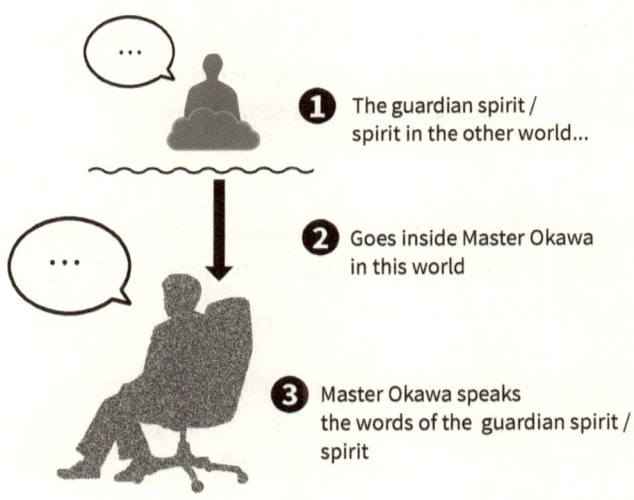

1. The guardian spirit / spirit in the other world...
2. Goes inside Master Okawa in this world
3. Master Okawa speaks the words of the guardian spirit / spirit

*For more about spiritual messages and a complete list of books in the Spiritual Interview Series, visit **okawabooks.com***

ABOUT HAPPY SCIENCE

Happy Science is a global movement that empowers individuals to find purpose and spiritual happiness and to share that happiness with their families, societies, and the world. With more than 12 million members around the world, Happy Science aims to increase awareness of spiritual truths and expand our capacity for love, compassion, and joy so that together we can create the kind of world we all wish to live in.

Activities at Happy Science are based on the Principles of Happiness (Love, Wisdom, Self-Reflection, and Progress). These principles embrace worldwide philosophies and beliefs, transcending boundaries of culture and religions.

> **Love** teaches us to give ourselves freely without expecting anything in return; it encompasses giving, nurturing, and forgiving.
>
> **Wisdom** leads us to the insights of spiritual truths, and opens us to the true meaning of life and the will of God (the universe, the highest power, Buddha).
>
> **Self-Reflection** brings a mindful, nonjudgmental lens to our thoughts and actions to help us find our truest selves—the essence of our souls—and deepen our connection to the highest power. It helps us attain a clean and peaceful mind and leads us to the right life path.

Progress emphasizes the positive, dynamic aspects of our spiritual growth—actions we can take to manifest and spread happiness around the world. It's a path that not only expands our soul growth, but also furthers the collective potential of the world we live in.

PROGRAMS AND EVENTS

The doors of Happy Science are open to all. We offer a variety of programs and events, including self-exploration and self-growth programs, spiritual seminars, meditation and contemplation sessions, study groups, and book events.

Our programs are designed to:
* Deepen your understanding of your purpose and meaning in life
* Improve your relationships and increase your capacity to love unconditionally
* Attain peace of mind, decrease anxiety and stress, and feel positive
* Gain deeper insights and a broader perspective on the world
* Learn how to overcome life's challenges
  ... and much more.

*For more information, visit **happy-science.org**.*

OUR ACTIVITIES

Happy Science does other various activities to provide support for those in need.

- **You Are An Angel! General Incorporated Association**
  Happy Science has a volunteer network in Japan that encourages and supports children with disabilities as well as their parents and guardians.

- **Never Mind School for Truancy**
  At 'Never Mind,' we support students who find it very challenging to attend schools in Japan. We also nurture their self-help spirit and power to rebound against obstacles in life based on Master Okawa's teachings and faith.

- **"Prevention Against Suicide" Campaign since 2003**
  A nationwide campaign to reduce suicides; over 20,000 people commit suicide every year in Japan. "The Suicide Prevention Website-Words of Truth for You-" presents spiritual prescriptions for worries such as depression, lost love, extramarital affairs, bullying and work-related problems, thereby saving many lives.

- **Support for Anti-bullying Campaigns**
  Happy Science provides support for a group of parents and guardians, Network to Protect Children from Bullying, a general incorporated foundation launched in Japan to end bullying, including those that can even be called a criminal offense. So far, the network received more than 5,000 cases and resolved 90% of them.

- **The Golden Age Scholarship**

    This scholarship is granted to students who can contribute greatly and bring a hopeful future to the world.

- **Success No.1**
    Buddha's Truth Afterschool Academy

    Happy Science has over 180 classrooms throughout Japan and in several cities around the world that focus on afterschool education for children. The education focuses on faith and morals in addition to supporting children's school studies.

- **Angel Plan V**

    For children under the age of kindergarten, Happy Science holds classes for nurturing healthy, positive, and creative boys and girls.

- **Future Stars Training Department**

    The Future Stars Training Department was founded within the Happy Science Media Division with the goal of nurturing talented individuals to become successful in the performing arts and entertainment industry.

- **New Star Production Co., Ltd.**
    ARI Production Co., Ltd.

    We have companies to nurture actors and actresses, artists, and vocalists. They are also involved in film production.

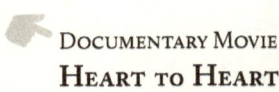
DOCUMENTARY MOVIE
HEART TO HEART

In this documentary movie, Happy Science University students visit these NPO activities to discover what salvation truly is, and on the meaning of life, through heart-to-heart interviews.

ABOUT HAPPY SCIENCE MOVIES

TWICEBORN

Coming to Theaters Fall 2020

2 Awards from 2 Countries!

SPAIN
**MADRID INTERNATIONAL FILM FESTIVAL 2020
BEST FOREIGN LANGUAGE FEATURE FILM**

**AWARENESS FILM FESTIVAL 2020
MERIT AWARD**

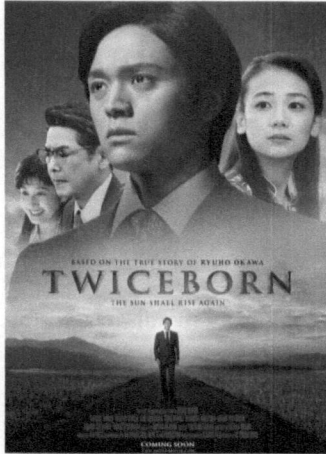

STORY Satoru Ichijo receives a message from the spiritual world and realizes his mission is to lead humankind to happiness. He became a successful businessman while publishing spiritual messages secretly, but the devil's temptation shakes his mind and...

LIVING IN THE AGE OF MIRACLES

A documentary film released in Aug. 2020

An inspirational documentary about two Japanese actors meeting people who experienced miracles in their lives. Through their quest, they find the key to working miracles and learn what "living in the age of miracles" truly means.

6 Awards from USA!

**WINNER
AWARD OF MERIT
SPECIAL MENTION
IMPACT DOCS AWARDS**

**GOLD AWARD
Documentary Feature**
International
Independent Film Awards
Spring 2020

**GOLD AWARD
Concept**
International
Independent Film Awards
Spring 2020

...and more!

IMMORTAL HERO `On VOD NOW`

Based on the true story of a man whose near death experience inspires him to choose life... and change the lives of millions.

40 Awards from 9 Countries!

SPAIN
BARCELONA INTERNATIONAL FILM FESTIVAL 2019
[THE CASTELL AWARDS]

SPAIN
MADRID INTERNATIONAL FILM FESTIVAL 2019
[BEST DIRECTOR OF A FOREIGN LANGUAGE FEATURE FILM]

ITALY
FLORENCE FILM AWARDS JUL 2019
[HONORABLE MENTION: FEATURE FILM]

USA
INDIE VISIONS FILM FESTIVAL JUL 2019 [WINNER (NARRATIVE FEATURE FILM)]

ITALY
FLORENCE FILM AWARDS JUL 2019
[BEST ORIGINAL SCREENPLAY]

ITALY
DIAMOND FILM AWARDS JUL 2019 [WINNER (NARRATIVE FEATURE FILM)]

...and more!

For more information, visit **www.immortal-hero.com**

THE REAL EXORCIST

55 Awards from 8 Countries!

STORY Tokyo —the most mystical city in the world where you find spiritual spots in the most unexpected places. Sayuri works as a part time waitress at a small coffee shop "Extra" where regular customers enjoy the authentic coffee that the owner brews. Meanwhile, Sayuri uses her supernatural powers to help those who are troubled by spiritual phenomena one after another. Through her special consultations, she touches the hearts of the people and helps them by showing the truths of the invisible world.

USA
GOLD REMI AWARD
53rd WorldFest Houston International Film Festival 2020

MONACO
BEST FEATURE FILM
17th Angel Film Awards 2020
Monaco International Film Festival

BEST FEMALE ACTOR
17th Angel Film Awards 2020
Monaco International Film Festival

NIGERIA
BEST FEATURE FILM
EKO International Film Festival 2020

BEST FEMALE SUPPORTING ACTOR
17th Angel Film Awards 2020
Monaco International Film Festival

BEST SUPPORTING ACTRESS
EKO International Film Festival 2020

BEST VISUAL EFFECTS
17th Angel Film Awards 2020
Monaco International Film Festival

...and more!

For more information, visit **www.realexorcistmovie.com**

CONTACT INFORMATION

Happy Science is a worldwide organization with faith centers around the globe. For a comprehensive list of centers, visit the worldwide directory at *happy-science.org*. The following are some of the many Happy Science locations:

UNITED STATES AND CANADA

New York
79 Franklin St., New York, NY 10013
Phone: 212-343-7972
Fax: 212-343-7973
Email: ny@happy-science.org
Website: happyscience-na.org

Los Angeles
1590 E. Del Mar Blvd., Pasadena, CA 91106
Phone: 626-395-7775
Fax: 626-395-7776
Email: la@happy-science.org
Website: happyscience-na.org

New Jersey
725 River Rd, #102B, Edgewater, NJ 07020
Phone: 201-313-0127
Fax: 201-313-0120
Email: nj@happy-science.org
Website: happyscience-na.org

Orange County
10231 Slater Ave., #204
Fountain Valley, CA 92708
Phone: 714-745-1140
Email: oc@happy-science.org
Website: happyscience-na.org

Florida
5208 8th St., St. Zephyrhills, FL 33542
Phone: 813-715-0000
Fax: 813-715-0010
Email: florida@happy-science.org
Website: happyscience-na.org

San Diego
7841 Balboa Ave., Suite #202
San Diego, CA 92111
Phone: 626-395-7775
Fax: 626-395-7776
E-mail: sandiego@happy-science.org
Website: happyscience-na.org

Atlanta
1874 Piedmont Ave., NE Suite 360-C
Atlanta, GA 30324
Phone: 404-892-7770
Email: atlanta@happy-science.org
Website: happyscience-na.org

Hawaii
Phone: 808-591-9772
Fax: 808-591-9776
Email: hi@happy-science.org
Website: happyscience-na.org

San Francisco
525 Clinton St.
Redwood City, CA 94062
Phone & Fax: 650-363-2777
Email: sf@happy-science.org
Website: happyscience-na.org

Kauai
3343 Kanakolu Street, Suite 5
Lihue, HI 96766, U.S.A.
Phone: 808-822-7007
Fax: 808-822-6007
Email: kauai-hi@happy-science.org
Website: kauai.happyscience-na.org

Toronto
845 The Queensway
Etobicoke ON M8Z 1N6 Canada
Phone: 1-416-901-3747
Email: toronto@happy-science.org
Website: happy-science.ca

Vancouver
#201-2607 East 49th Avenue
Vancouver, BC, V5S 1J9, Canada
Phone: 1-604-437-7735
Fax: 1-604-437-7764
Email: vancouver@happy-science.org
Website: happy-science.ca

INTERNATIONAL

Tokyo
1-6-7 Togoshi, Shinagawa
Tokyo, 142-0041 Japan
Phone: 81-3-6384-5770
Fax: 81-3-6384-5776
Email: tokyo@happy-science.org
Website: happy-science.org

Seoul
74, Sadang-ro 27-gil,
Dongjak-gu, Seoul, Korea
Phone: 82-2-3478-8777
Fax: 82-2-3478-9777
Email: korea@happy-science.org
Website: happyscience-korea.org

London
3 Margaret St.
London,W1W 8RE United Kingdom
Phone: 44-20-7323-9255
Fax: 44-20-7323-9344
Email: eu@happy-science.org
Website: happyscience-uk.org

Taipei
No. 89, Lane 155, Dunhua N. Road
Songshan District, Taipei City 105, Taiwan
Phone: 886-2-2719-9377
Fax: 886-2-2719-5570
Email: taiwan@happy-science.org
Website: happyscience-tw.org

Sydney
516 Pacific Hwy, Lane Cove North,
NSW 2066, Australia
Phone: 61-2-9411-2877
Fax: 61-2-9411-2822
Email: sydney@happy-science.org

Malaysia
No 22A, Block 2, Jalil Link Jalan Jalil Jaya 2,
Bukit Jalil 57000, Kuala Lumpur, Malaysia
Phone: 60-3-8998-7877
Fax: 60-3-8998-7977
Email: malaysia@happy-science.org
Website: happyscience.org.my

Brazil Headquarters
Rua. Domingos de Morais 1154,
Vila Mariana, Sao Paulo SP
CEP 04009-002, Brazil
Phone: 55-11-5088-3800
Fax: 55-11-5088-3806
Email: sp@happy-science.org
Website: happyscience.com.br

Nepal
Kathmandu Metropolitan City Ward
No. 15,
Ring Road, Kimdol,
Sitapaila Kathmandu, Nepal
Phone: 97-714-272931
Email: nepal@happy-science.org

Jundiai
Rua Congo, 447, Jd. Bonfiglioli
Jundiai-CEP, 13207-340
Phone: 55-11-4587-5952
Email: jundiai@happy-science.org

Uganda
Plot 877 Rubaga Road, Kampala
P.O. Box 34130, Kampala, Uganda
Phone: 256-79-4682-121
Email: uganda@happy-science.org
Website: happyscience-uganda.org

ABOUT HAPPINESS REALIZATION PARTY

The Happiness Realization Party (HRP) was founded in May 2009 by Master Ryuho Okawa as part of the Happy Science Group to offer concrete and proactive solutions to the current issues such as military threats from North Korea and China and the long-term economic recession. HRP aims to implement drastic reforms of the Japanese government, thereby bringing peace and prosperity to Japan. To accomplish this, HRP proposes two key policies:

1) Strengthening the national security and the Japan-U.S. alliance, which plays a vital role in the stability of Asia.

2) Improving the Japanese economy by implementing drastic tax cuts, taking monetary easing measures and creating new major industries.

HRP advocates that Japan should offer a model of a religious nation that allows diverse values and beliefs to coexist, and that contributes to global peace.

*For more information, visit **en.hr-party.jp***

ABOUT IRH PRESS

IRH Press Co., Ltd., based in Tokyo, was founded in 1987 as a publishing division of Happy Science. IRH Press publishes religious and spiritual books, journals, magazines and also operates broadcast and film production enterprises. For more information, visit *okawabooks.com*.

Follow us on:
Facebook: Okawa Books   **Twitter:** Okawa Books
Goodreads: Ryuho Okawa   **Instagram:** OkawaBooks
Pinterest: Okawa Books

RYUHO OKAWA'S LAWS SERIES

The Laws Series is an annual volume of books that are mainly comprised of Ryuho Okawa's lectures on various topics that highlight principles and guidelines for the activities of Happy Science every year. *The Laws of the Sun*, the first publication of the Laws Series, ranked in the annual best-selling list in Japan. Since then, all of the Laws Series' titles have ranked in the annual best-selling list for more than two decades, setting sociocultural trends in Japan and around the world.

THE TRILOGY

The first three volumes of the Laws Series, *The Laws of the Sun*, *The Golden Laws*, and *The Nine Dimensions* make a trilogy that completes the basic framework of the teachings of God's Truths. *The Laws of the Sun* discusses the structure of God's Laws, *The Golden Laws* expounds on the doctrine of time, and *The Nine Dimensions* reveals the nature of space.

BOOKS BY RYUHO OKAWA

The 26th Laws Series

THE LAWS OF STEEL

LIVING A LIFE OF RESILIENCE, CONFIDENCE AND PROSPERITY

Paperback • 256 pages • $16.95
ISBN: 978-1-942125-65-5

This book is a compilation of six lectures that Ryuho Okawa gave in 2018 and 2019, each containing passionate messages for us to open a brighter future. This powerful and inspiring book will not only show us the ways to achieve true happiness and prosperity, but also the ways to solve many global issues we now face. It presents us with wisdom that is based on a spiritual perspective, and a new design for our future society. Through this book, we can overcome differences in values and create a peaceful world, thereby ushering in a Golden Age.

> **Chapter list**
> *1* The Mindset to Invite Prosperity
> *2* The Law of Cause and Effect
> *3* Fulfilling *Noblesse Oblige*
> *4* Be Confident in Your Life
> *5* A Savior's Wish
> *6* The Power to Make Miracles

---

*For a complete list of books, visit **okawabooks.com***

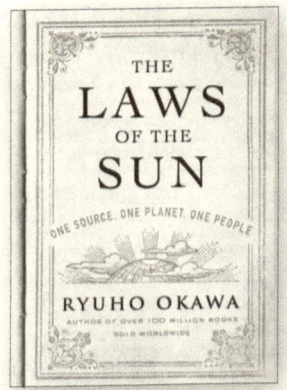

THE LAWS OF THE SUN
ONE SOURCE, ONE PLANET, ONE PEOPLE

Paperback • 288 pages • $15.95
ISBN: 978-1-942125-43-3

IMAGINE IF YOU COULD ASK GOD why He created this world and what spiritual laws He used to shape us—and everything around us. If we could understand His designs and intentions, we could discover what our goals in life should be and whether our actions move us closer to those goals or farther away.

At a young age, a spiritual calling prompted Ryuho Okawa to outline what he innately understood to be universal truths for all humankind. In *The Laws of the Sun*, Okawa outlines these laws of the universe and provides a road map for living one's life with greater purpose and meaning.

In this powerful book, Ryuho Okawa reveals the transcendent nature of consciousness and the secrets of our multidimensional universe and our place in it. By understanding the different stages of love and following the Buddhist Eightfold Path, he believes we can speed up our eternal process of development. *The Laws of the Sun* shows the way to realize true happiness—a happiness that continues from this world through the other.

For a complete list of books, visit **okawabooks.com**

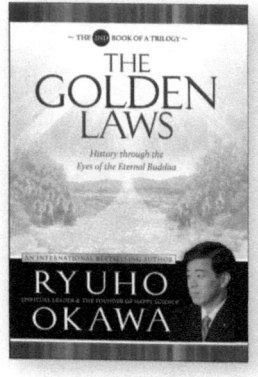

THE GOLDEN LAWS
HISTORY THROUGH THE EYES OF THE ETERNAL BUDDHA

Paperback • 201 pages • $14.95
ISBN: 978-1-941779-81-1

Throughout history, Great Guiding Spirits of Light have been present on Earth in both the East and the West at crucial points in human history to further our spiritual development. *The Golden Laws* reveals how Divine Plan has been unfolding on Earth, and outlines 5,000 years of the secret history of humankind. Once we understand the true course of history, through past, present and into the future, we cannot help but become aware of the significance of our spiritual mission in the present age.

THE NINE DIMENSIONS
UNVEILING THE LAWS OF ETERNITY

Paperback • 168 pages • $15.95
ISBN: 978-0-982698-56-3

This book is a window into the mind of our loving God, who designed this world and the vast, wondrous world of our afterlife as a school with many levels through which our souls learn and grow. When the religions and cultures of the world discover the truth of their common spiritual origin, they will be inspired to accept their differences, come together under faith in God, and build an era of harmony and peaceful progress on Earth.

---

*For a complete list of books, visit **okawabooks.com***

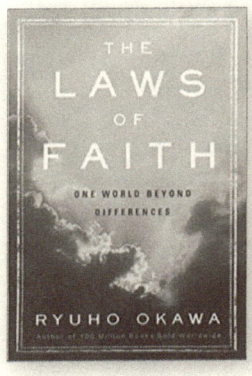

The Laws of Faith
One World Beyond Differences

Paperback • 208 pages • $15.95
ISBN: 978-1-942125-34-1

Ryuho Okawa preaches at the core of a new universal religion from various angles while integrating logical and spiritual viewpoints in mind with current world situations. This book offers us the key to accept diversities beyond differences in ethnicity, religion, race, gender, descent, and so on, harmonize the individuals and nations and create a world filled with peace and prosperity.

The Essence of Buddha
The Path to Enlightenment

Paperback • 208 pages • $14.95
ISBN: 978-1-942125-06-8

In this book, Ryuho Okawa imparts in simple and accessible language his wisdom about the essence of Shakyamuni Buddha's philosophy of life and enlightenment—teachings that have been inspiring people all over the world for over 2,500 years. By offering a new perspective on core Buddhist thoughts that have long been cloaked in mystique, Okawa brings these teachings to life for modern people. *The Essence of Buddha* distills a way of life that anyone can practice to achieve a life of self-growth, compassionate living, and true happiness.

---

*For a complete list of books, visit **okawabooks.com***

THE LAWS OF HAPPINESS
LOVE, WISDOM, SELF-REFLECTION AND PROGRESS

Paperback • 264 pages • $16.95
ISBN: 978-1-942125-70-9

This book endeavors to answer the question, "What is true happiness?" This milestone text introduces four distinct principles, based on the "Laws of Mind" and sourced from Okawa's real-world experience, to guide readers towards sustainable happiness. Okawa's four "Principles of Happiness" present an easy, yet profound framework to ground this rapidly advanced and highly competitive society. In practice, Okawa outlines pragmatic steps to revitalize our ambition to lead a happier and meaningful life.

THE LAWS OF JUSTICE
HOW WE CAN SOLVE WORLD CONFLICTS AND BRING PEACE

Paperback • 208 pages • $15.95
ISBN: 978-1-942125-05-1

This book shows what global justice is from a comprehensive perspective of the Supreme God. Becoming aware of this view will let us embrace differences in beliefs, recognize other people's divine nature, and love and forgive one another. It will also become the key to solving the issues we face, whether they're religious, political, societal, economic, or academic, and help the world become a better and safer world for all of us living today.

---

*For a complete list of books, visit **okawabooks.com***

Spiritual Interviews with the Guardian Spirits of Biden and Trump

Paperback • 200 pages • $13.95
ISBN: 978-1-943869-92-3

The 2020 U.S. presidential election will be a turning point in history. In this book, we spiritually closed in on the true thoughts of Biden and Trump to get a forecast of the presidential election. In short, China could become the next hegemonic state if Biden is elected the president. Who you vote for could change people's lives, for better or worse.

Love for the Future

Building One World of Freedom and Democracy Under God's Truth

Paperback • 312 pages • $15.95
ISBN: 978-1-942125-60-0

This is a compilation of select international lectures given by Ryuho Okawa during his (ongoing) global missionary tours. While conflicting values of justice exist, this book espouses freedom and democracy are vital principles for global unification that will resolutely foster peace and shared prosperity, if adopted universally.

For a complete list of books, visit **okawabooks.com**

The Real Exorcist
Attain Wisdom to Conquer Evil

Paperback • 208 pages • $16.95
ISBN:978-1-942125-67-9

This is a profound spiritual text backed by the author's nearly 40 years of real-life experience with spiritual phenomena. In it, Okawa teaches how we may discern and overcome our negative tendencies, by acquiring the right knowledge, mindset and lifestyle.

The Novel Coronavirus Originated in China: Lessons for Humankind
Spiritual messages from Shibasaburo Kitasato and R. A. Goal

Paperback • 228 pages • $13.95
ISBN: 978-1-943869-88-6

This book records spiritual messages from a bacteriologist and a space being. They disclose many truths about the novel coronavirus pandemic, such as China's hidden secrets, what the future holds, and hopeful messages for humanity. Only when humanity learns what we are to learn from this pandemic, can we escape this worldwide crisis and create a new age.

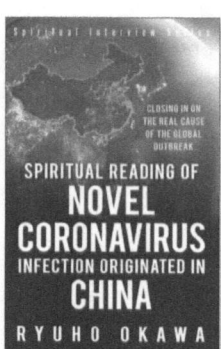

Spiritual Reading of Novel Coronavirus Infection Originated in China
Closing in on the real cause of the global outbreak

Paperback • 278 pages • $13.95
ISBN: 978-1-943869-77-0

This worldwide pandemic is not a mere act of nature nor a coincidence, but rather, heaven's warning to humanity, especially China. Through this book, you can find out "the immunity" against the novel coronavirus, among other shocking truths.

---

*For a complete list of books, visit **okawabooks.com***

JESUS CHRIST'S ANSWERS TO THE CORONAVIRUS PANDEMIC

Paperback • 204 pages • $11.95
ISBN: 978-1-943869-81-7

In this book, the spirit of Jesus answers the causes, prospects, and coping strategies for the novel coronavirus pandemic. Instead of hoping for the development of an effective vaccine to come soon, we should use our spiritual power to defeat the evil thoughts that spiritually possess this virus. It's a book for all who believe in Jesus.

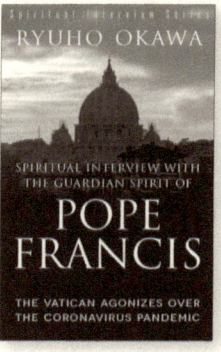

SPIRITUAL INTERVIEW WITH THE GUARDIAN SPIRIT OF POPE FRANCIS

THE VATICAN AGONIZES OVER THE CORONAVIRUS PANDEMIC

Paperback • 268 pages • $13.95
ISBN: 978-1-943869-84-8

In this book, the guardian spirit of Pope Francis confesses his hopelessness, goodwill, and limit as a human being amid the ongoing coronavirus pandemic. Are his prayers heard by Jesus? By also reading *Jesus Christ's Answers to the Coronavirus Pandemic*, you will be able to understand the true will of Jesus and the faith in true God.

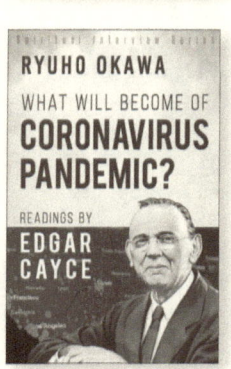

WHAT WILL BECOME OF CORONAVIRUS PANDEMIC?

READINGS BY EDGAR CAYCE

Paperback • 86 pages • $9.95
ISBN: 978-1-943869-82-4

Edgar Cayce, now a spirit in heaven, tells us that the novel coronavirus infection is likely to spread even further, but he also teaches us the truth behind it and how to deal with it. But you, yourself, can gain the power to defeat the novel coronavirus. Here is your light of hope.

For a complete list of books, visit okawabooks.com

JOHN LENNON'S MESSAGE FROM HEAVEN
On the Spirit of Love and Peace, Music,
and the Incredible Secret of His Soul

THE NEW RESURRECTION
My Miraculous Story of Overcoming Illness and Death

THE ROYAL ROAD OF LIFE
Beginning Your Path of Inner Peace, Virtue, and a Life of Purpose

THE LAWS OF GREAT ENLIGHTENMENT
Always Walk with Buddha

THE HELL YOU NEVER KNEW
And How to Avoid Going There

MESSAGES FROM HEAVEN
What Jesus, Buddha, Moses, and Muhammad Would Say Today

HEALING FROM WITHIN
Life-Changing Keys to Calm, Spiritual, and Healthy Living

BASICS OF EXORCISM
How to Protect You and Your Family from Evil Spirits

SPIRITUAL WORLD 101
A Guide to a Spiritually Happy Life

---

*For a complete list of books, visit **okawabooks.com***

MUSIC BY RYUHO OKAWA

CD available at Happy Science local temples

a composition for repelling the Coronavirus

We have been granted this music from our Lord. It will repel away the novel Coronavirus originated in China. Experience this magnificent powerful music.

Search on YouTube

the thunder repelling

for a short ad!

 Available online
Spotify   iTunes   Amazon

www.ingramcontent.com/pod-product-compliance
Lightning Source LLC
Chambersburg PA
CBHW030150100526
44592CB00009B/204